Test Prep

Grade 7

FlashKids

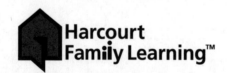

© 2005 by Flash Kids
Adapted from *Test Best for Test Prep, Level G*
© 1999 by Harcourt Achieve
Licensed under special arrangement with Harcourt Achieve.

Production by Creative Media Applications

ISBN: 978-1-4114-0403-8

Please submit all inquiries to FlashKid@bn.com

Printed and bound in China

Flash Kids
A Division of Barnes & Noble
122 Fifth Avenue
New York, NY 10011

TABLE OF CONTENTS

FOR TEST-SMART PARENTS

As you know, standardized tests are an important part of your child's school career. These tests are created by your state's education department and set to its standards of learning for each grade level. These tests are valuable tools that measure how much your child knows in the areas of reading and math. *Test Prep: Grade 7* is designed to familiarize your child with test formats and directions, teach test-taking strategies, and provide practice in skill areas that most states consider important. This workbook will also help your child review the basic skills taught in the seventh grade.

Preparation is the key to helping your child become test-smart. Practicing basic skills in a testing situation can help ensure that your child's scores reflect his or her understanding of the material presented in school. Test-smart students:

- are comfortable in the testing environment;
- know how to approach different kinds of test questions;
- apply knowledge to a variety of test formats;
- use time wisely during tests.

Completing the practice exercises and tests in this workbook can help your child relax and feel ready as test day approaches. This practice also provides a review of the essential skills that will help your child with coursework during the school year.

ABOUT THIS WORKBOOK

Test Prep: Grade 7 is divided into three helpful sections. Practice exercises and mini-tests introduce and review basic test-taking skills. Longer practice tests that mirror the actual tests your child will encounter at school appear at the end of the book.

- **Unit 1: Test-Taking Strategies**
  These pages help your child learn essential strategies to use during any standardized test. You might read these pages together with your child. Talk about which strategies your child has used before and which ones are new.

- **Units 2–7: Mini-Tests**
  Each unit focuses on a subject found on standardized tests: reading comprehension, reading vocabulary, mathematics, problem solving, and language. These mini-tests help your child learn specific test strategies. Each unit concludes with a unit test that covers all of the skills in the unit's lessons.

- **Units 8–11: Practice Tests**
  These longer practice tests help your child apply test-taking skills in a realistic testing environment. Your child will use the Answer Sheet at the back of this book to record responses. Familiarizing your child with the testing experience can lessen feelings of intimidation during any type of school assessment.

Throughout the mini-tests, hints and Test Tips will draw your child's attention to useful ways to approach individual problems. Test Tips do not appear in the final practice tests, which reflect realistic testing situations.

FOUR PRINCIPLES OF TEST-TAKING

These tests help your child develop four important skills that are crucial in testing situations. Familiarize yourself with these goals in order to support your child's development of these skills.

USING TIME WISELY

All standardized tests are timed. Your child needs to understand how to manage time wisely. Review these strategies together:

- Work rapidly but comfortably.
- Do not spend too much time on any one question.
- Mark items to return to if there is enough time.
- Use any remaining time to review answers.
- Use a watch to keep track of time.

AVOIDING ERRORS

Your child can practice these strategies when choosing the correct answers on standardized tests:

- Pay careful attention to directions.
- Determine what is being asked.
- Mark answers in the appropriate place.
- Check all answers.
- Do not make stray marks on the answer sheet.

REASONING

Standardized tests require your child to think logically when answering each question. These strategies can help your child think through each question before choosing the best answer:

- Before answering a question, read the entire question or passage and all the answer choices.
- Restate questions and answer choices in your own words.
- Use logic and reasoning skills to test answer choices and eliminate incorrect answers.
- Apply skills learned in class and practice situations.

GUESSING

Many standardized tests take away points for incorrect answers. Random guessing will not improve your child's test scores, but educated guessing can help your child score points when the correct answer is not immediately clear.

- Try to answer all of the questions within the allotted time. Do not spend too much time on a question that seems hard.
- Eliminate answers that you know are incorrect. If you cannot do this, skip the question.
- Compare the remaining answers. Restate the question, and then choose the answer that seems most correct.

Daily encouragement and support for learning will help your child feel confident and secure. Every student needs much experience with reading and exposure to a wide variety of reading material. The school curriculum is carefully designed to teach skills your child needs to become a proficient learner. Your home environment is another essential part of the education equation. Here are some ways you can help your child year-round.

CREATE A SUCCESSFUL STUDY SPACE

A quiet, clean, and cheerful study space will help your child develop strong study habits. Provide a study area with an open workspace. Make sure that writing supplies like paper and pencils are nearby, as well as tools like a calculator, ruler, scissors, glue, and a dictionary. You might also create files or boxes to store your child's work. Make separate files for finished works and works in progress. Help your child create and follow a study schedule.

BE A HOMEWORK HELPER

Talk about homework assignments with your child. Your questions can help your child focus on what is important about the task or project. Your interest in schoolwork will encourage your child's enthusiasm and dedication. Check in while your child is working to see if you can answer any questions or help find solutions. Just letting your child know that you care can promote active learning.

USE THE INTERNET EFFECTIVELY

Many seventh graders use the Internet as a reference source. Monitor your child's use of the Internet, and together decide if a Web site probably contains information that is correct. Look for Internet sites sponsored by educational organizations (many of which have URLs that end with .edu). Remind your child that sites written by other students may not have been checked carefully for accuracy. Your child should try to back up important information with library sources, such as encyclopedias and other books.

PRACTICE WITH A CALCULATOR

Many standardized tests allow students to use calculators. Make sure you have a calculator at home that is in good working condition. Calculators do not replace learning math skills. However, using calculators accurately is essential in many real-life situations. Encourage your child to use a calculator to complete homework or to help with household computations.

TALK ABOUT TESTS

Find out from your child's teacher when standardized tests will be given during the school year. Mark the dates on your calendar so that both you and your child know when test day approaches. Try not to schedule big activities for the night before a test.

To prepare for the yearly standardized test, score your child's work in this workbook together. Then talk about questions that were easy, hard, or tricky. Review any items answered incorrectly and work together to understand why another answer is better.

A Good Night's Sleep

Your child will be more relaxed and alert after a full night of sleep. Some physical exercise before dinner can relieve feelings of stress. Do not place too much emphasis on the upcoming test, but answer any questions your child may have and provide reassurance that your child is ready for the test. Reminders of what to expect may lower anxiety. Help your child choose clothing for the next day, and have it ready so there is no last-minute hunting in the morning.

Food for Thought

Studies show a direct link between eating a balanced breakfast and student performance. Students who eat a good breakfast are alert in class, concentrate well, and recall information. These skills are useful at any time of the year, but are especially helpful on test day. To make sure your child eats a balanced breakfast, wake up early enough to leave plenty of time for a relaxed meal together.

Support Your Child

Remind your child that standardized tests measure learning. They do not measure intelligence. Supportive parents expect their children to do their best. Do not set specific goals or offer rewards for high scores. Instead, assure your child that you will be happy with a positive and wholehearted effort. Doing one's best is what really counts!

AFTER THE TEST

When your child comes home, discuss the testing experience. Do not focus on the test score. Instead, use the opportunity to reassure your child and talk about test-taking strategies. Every test is an opportunity to improve. Ask your child which strategies were especially useful. To keep the mood relaxed at home, choose a fun activity to help your child unwind after the test.

When the test scores arrive, remember to keep the results in perspective. Unless specified, most tests do not measure intelligence. A test score simply measures how well your child knows the materials and skills covered on that specific test.

Be sure to talk about the test score with your child. Remind your child that no single test score gives a complete picture of how much someone knows. Help your child set goals to maintain or improve test scores in the future. Always praise your child for working hard on a test. Test scores might suggest that your child needs improvement in a specific skill or subject. Talk with your child's teacher to find ways to support your child's growth in a particular area.

GET READY FOR TESTS

WHAT ARE STANDARDIZED TESTS?

You will take many different tests while at school. A standardized test is a special test that your state gives to every student in your grade. These tests are designed to find out how much you know about subjects like reading and math. They may not be fun, but they do not have to be a nightmare. This workbook can help you prepare!

WHAT CAN YOU EXPECT ON A STANDARDIZED TEST?

All standardized tests are different, but they do have some things in common.

- **Multiple-Choice Questions**
  Most of these tests use multiple-choice questions. You have to pick the best answer from four or five choices. You usually indicate your choice on an answer sheet by filling in or darkening a circle next to the correct answer.

- **Time Limits**
  Standardized tests all have time limits. It is best to answer as many questions as possible before you run out of time. But do not let the time limit make you nervous. Use it to help you keep going at a good pace.

- **Short Answers and Essays**
  Some standardized tests have questions that require writing an answer. Sometimes the answer is a word or a sentence. Other times you will write a paragraph or an essay. Always read directions carefully to find out how much writing is required.

HOW CAN THIS BOOK HELP?

Everyone gets a little nervous when taking a test. This book can make test-taking easier by providing helpful tips and practice tests. You will learn strategies that will help you find the best answers. You will also review math, reading, and grammar skills that are commonly needed on standardized tests. Here are some hints for using this book.

- Work in a quiet place. When you take a test at school, the room is very quiet. Try to duplicate that feeling at home. Sit in a chair at a desk or table, just as you would in school.

- Finish one test at a time. Do not try to finish all of the tests in this book in one session. It is better to complete just one activity at a time. You will learn more if you stop at the end of a practice test to think about the completed questions.

- Ask questions. Talk with a family member or a friend if you find a question you do not understand. These practice tests give you the chance to check your own answers.

- Look for the Test Tips throughout this workbook. They provide hints and ideas to help you find the best answers.

How to Be Test Smart

A test-smart student knows what to do when it is test-taking time. You might not know all the answers, but you will feel relaxed and focused when you take tests. Your test scores will be accurate. They will provide a snapshot of what you have learned during the school year. Here is how you can become test-smart!

Things You Can Do All Year

The best way to get ready for tests is to pay attention in school and keep up with all of your assignments. Your school curriculum is designed to teach important information and skills. However, learning does not have to stop in the classroom. Here are some ways you can become a year-round learner.

- Do your schoolwork. Standardized tests measure how much you have learned. If you keep up with your schoolwork, your test scores will reflect all the things you have learned.

- Practice smart study habits. Most people study best when they work in a quiet, clean area. Keep your study area neat. Make sure you have a calculator, dictionary, paper, and pencils nearby.

- Read a wide variety of materials, including all sorts of fiction and nonfiction. Your school or local librarian can suggest books you might not have considered reading. Read newspapers and magazines to find out about current events.

- Be a critical reader. Evaluate the quality and accuracy of everything you read. Remember that information on the Internet and in other media sources may or may not be true. It is up to you to decide which sources you can trust.

- Practice. This book is a great start to help you get ready for test day. It provides practice for all the important skills on the tests.

How to Do Your Best on Test Day

Your teacher will announce a standardized test day in advance. Follow these tips to help you succeed on the big day.

- Plan a quiet night before a test. Trying to study or memorize facts at this point might make you nervous. Enjoy a relaxing evening instead.

- Go to bed on time. You need to be well rested before the test.

- Eat a balanced breakfast. Your body needs fuel to keep your energy high during a test. Eat foods that provide long-term energy, like eggs, yogurt, or fruit. Skip the sugary cereals—the energy they give does not last very long.

- Wear comfortable clothes. Choose an outfit that makes you feel relaxed.

- Do not worry about the other students or your friends. Everyone works at different speeds. Pay attention to answering the questions in a steady fashion. It does not matter when someone else finishes the test.

- Relax. Take a few deep breaths to help you relax. Hold your pencil comfortably and do not squeeze it. Take a break every so often to wiggle your fingers and stretch your hand.

Here are some hints and strategies to help you feel comfortable with any test. Remember these ideas while taking the tests in this book.

READ THE DIRECTIONS

This sounds obvious, but every year students lose points because they assume they know the right thing to do—and they are wrong! Make sure you read and understand the directions for every test. Never assume you know what to do. Always begin by reading the directions. They will focus your attention on finding the right answers.

READ THE ANSWERS

Read the answers—ALL the answers—for a multiple-choice question, even if you think the first one is correct. Test writers sometimes put trick answers in the first or second option. You can avoid falling for this trap by reading every answer every time.

PREVIEW THE QUESTIONS

Scan each section. This will give you information about the questions. You also can see how many questions there are in the section. Do not spend too much time doing this. A quick glance will provide helpful information without making you nervous.

USE YOUR TIME WISELY

Always follow test rules. On most standardized tests, you can work on only one section at a time. Do not skip ahead or return to another section. If you finish early, go back and check your answers in that section.

- Before the test begins, find out if you can write in the test booklet. If so, add a small circle or star next to those questions that you find difficult. If time allows, come back to these questions before time is up for that section.

- Try not to spend too much time on one question. Skip a difficult question and try to answer it later. Be careful, though! You need to skip that question's number on your answer sheet. When you answer the next question, make sure you carefully fill in or darken the circle for the correct question.

- When finishing a section, look at your answer sheet. Did you answer every question for the section? Erase any extra marks on your answer sheet. Make sure you did not mark two answers for one question.

- Set your own schedule for writing exams. If you have 45 minutes to write an essay, you might decide to spend 10 minutes prewriting, 25 minutes drafting your essay, and 10 minutes revising and proofreading it.

THINK BEFORE YOU SWITCH

When you check your answers, you might be tempted to change one or more of them. In most cases, your first answer is probably the best choice. Ask yourself why you want to make a change. If you have a good reason, go ahead and pick a new answer. For example, you might have misread the question. If you cannot think of a specific reason, it is probably best to stick with your original answer choice.

MAKE AN EDUCATED GUESS

Most standardized tests take away points for wrong answers. It might be wise to skip a question if you have no idea about the answer. Leave the answer blank and move on to the next question. But if you can eliminate one or more of the answers, guessing can be a great strategy. In other words, random guessing will not help, but smart guessing can improve your test scores.

- Read every answer choice.

- Eliminate as many answers as possible.

- Try rereading or restating the question to find the best answer.

- If you decide to skip a question, make sure you leave the answer space for that question blank and move on to the next space when recording the answer to the next question.

FILL IN THE BLANKS

Many tests include fill-in-the-blank questions. The blank is usually in the middle or at the end of a sentence. Use these steps to answer a fill-in-the-blank question.

- Begin with the first answer choice. Read the sentence with that word or group of words in place of the blank. Ask yourself, "Does this answer make sense?"

- Then try filling in the blank with each of the other answer choices. Also, use the other words in the sentence as clues to help you decide the correct choice.

- Choose the best answer.

LOOK FOR CLUE WORDS

When you read test questions, watch for *clue words* that provide important information. Here are some words that make a difference.

- NOT: Many questions ask you to find the answer that is not true. These questions can be tricky. Slow down and think about the meaning of the question. Then pick the one answer that is not true.

- ALWAYS, NEVER, ALL, NONE, ONLY: These words limit a statement. They often make a generally true statement into a false one.

- SOMETIMES, SOME, MOST, MANY, OFTEN, GENERALLY: These words make a statement more believable. You will find them in many correct answers.

- BEST, MOST LIKELY, SAME, OPPOSITE, PROBABLY: These words change the meaning of a sentence. You often can use them to eliminate choices.

TEST TIP

Be sure to look for the Test Tips throughout this workbook. They will give you more test-taking strategies and specific help with certain subject areas.

SIX READING SKILLS

SKILL 1: DETERMINING WORD MEANINGS

Prefixes and suffixes are parts of some words. A *prefix* appears at the beginning of a word. A *suffix* appears at the end of a word. Both prefixes and suffixes affect the meaning of the word. Readers can use them to help figure out the meaning of a word.

Both of the teenagers had a problem with their mother. They were good students, helped around the house, and did their own laundry. But she remained hypercritical.

1 **In this selection, the word hypercritical means —**

    A hysterical.

    B underactive.

    C overly critical.

    D under pressure.

Hint: "Hyper-" is a prefix that means too much.

Bob went to look at the apartment with the realtor. The neighborhood looked nice enough, and there were lots of stores within walking distance. They walked up a flight of stairs outside; it was the first apartment on the right. When they opened the door, Bob could not believe how spacious the rooms were.

2 **In this paragraph, the word spacious means —**

    F large.

    G crowded.

    H dirty.

    J sparkling.

Hint: The suffix "-ious" means characterized by.

He had said some pretty bad things to the teacher when he saw her after school. Maybe he had just had enough of being called upon in class when he was unprepared. In retrospect, however, he was sorry he had lost his temper. He vowed to meet with his teacher the next morning to make things right.

3 **In this paragraph, what does the word retrospect mean?**

looking back in the past/retracing your steps.

Hint: "Retro-" is a prefix that means backwards.

Answers
1 Ⓐ Ⓑ Ⓒ Ⓓ   **2** Ⓕ Ⓖ Ⓗ Ⓙ

SKILL 1: DETERMINING WORD MEANINGS

Sometimes you can figure out the meaning of a new word by using the words around it as clues.

A woman in Australia and a woman in England were pen pals for a long time. Their correspondence lasted over 75 years.

1 **In this paragraph, the word correspondence means —**

   A letter writing.

   B friends.

   C phone calls.

   D mailbox.

Hint: You get a clue as to what the word correspondence *means in the first sentence.*

At the beach, there is a contest for building castles from the sand. Some of the castles are very elaborate. They have towers, windows, and even bridges.

2 **In this paragraph, the word elaborate means —**

   F sandy.

   G short.

   H plain.

   J fancy.

Hint: You get a clue as to what the word elaborate *means by reading the description of the castles in the last sentence.*

Animals that live in the desert are well protected. Their small bodies help them escape the heat that scorches the ground. Some animals stay in tunnels when the hot sun beats down.

3 **In this paragraph, the word scorches means —**

_____

_____

_____

_____

_____

_____

_____

Hint: You get a clue as to what scorches *means by the numerous references to heat.*

TEST TIP

Some vocabulary questions provide context clues. When you are asked to find the meaning of a vocabulary word in a passage, you will usually find at least one clear clue about the word's meaning. These items test your ability to use reasoning and find the best answer. The writers do not expect you to know the word's meaning. Take time to read the surrounding sentences and think about what they tell about the italicized or underlined word.

GO ON

Answers
1 Ⓐ Ⓑ © Ⓓ   **2** Ⓕ Ⓖ Ⓗ Ⓙ

SKILL 1: DETERMINING WORD MEANINGS

Specialized or technical words are words used in specific subjects, such as science and social studies. Readers can use all the other information in the text to help determine the meaning of such words.

In 1902, a man asked a woman to marry him. She said, "Yes." They decided to wait a few years before they got married. They finally got around to <u>matrimony</u> in 1969.

1   In this paragraph, the word <u>matrimony</u> means —

    A   talking.

    B   trying.

    C   marrying.

    D   dying.

Hint: You get a clue as to what the word <u>matrimony</u> means by reading the many references to marriage throughout.

In 1980, someone threw a grape more than three hundred feet. A man caught the grape in his mouth. The <u>site</u> of this event was a football field in Louisiana.

2   In this paragraph, the word <u>site</u> means –

    F   toss.

    G   place.

    H   time.

    J   game.

Hint: <u>Site</u> is a technical word. You get a clue as to what it means in the sentence in which it appears.

Pepper was once very rare. Armies seized it when they took over a city. In the fifth century, the Romans had to give three thousand pounds of it to enemies. Besides pepper, the winners also took gold, silver, and silk as part of their <u>booty</u>.

3   In this paragraph, the word <u>booty</u> means —

_____

_____

_____

_____

_____

_____

Hint: <u>Booty</u> is a technical word. You get a clue as to what it means from reading the entire paragraph.

TEST TIP

Technical words have special meanings in some subject areas. For example, you might have a lot of *work* every day, but in science, the word *work* describes the energy used when a force moves an object. When you read a science or social studies passage, watch for unusual meanings of familiar words.

GO ON ➤

Answers
1 Ⓐ Ⓑ Ⓒ Ⓓ   2 Ⓕ Ⓖ Ⓗ Ⓙ

A word can have different meanings depending on when and how you use it. Readers can figure out the correct meaning of a word by reading the entire passage.

No one could call him dishonest. If he found a wallet with $100 in it, he would return it to its owner. He was a just man.

1   In this passage, the word just means —

A   rich.

B   phony.

C   only.

D   righteous.

Hint: Read the whole passage to determine what kind of man he was.

Wanda came into the room looking for Rochelle. I told her that Rochelle had just left.

2   In this passage, the word just means —

F   only.

G   a very short time ago.

H   never.

J   a very long time ago.

Hint: You must read the whole selection to determine the meaning.

As we walked through it, I saw how beautiful the estate of the foreign diplomat was. Each building within the compound was more beautiful than the last.

3   In this passage, the word compound means —

A   combination of elements.

B   enclosed space containing buildings.

C   architectural drawing.

D   painting.

Hint: Read both sentences to determine the meaning.

The chemist invented a new compound. He hoped this mixture would give him the recognition he wanted.

4   In this passage, the word compound means —

F   combination of elements.

G   enclosed space.

H   architectural drawing.

J   painting.

Hint: You must read both sentences to determine the meaning.

STOP

Answers

1 Ⓐ Ⓑ Ⓒ Ⓓ   2 Ⓕ Ⓖ Ⓗ Ⓙ   3 Ⓐ Ⓑ Ⓒ Ⓓ   4 Ⓕ Ⓖ Ⓗ Ⓙ

SKILL 2: IDENTIFYING SUPPORTING IDEAS

Some facts and details are important. By noticing and remembering them, you will understand better what the passage is about.

Many hundreds of years ago, a monk from India traveled to China. He began teaching people special movements to train the mind and body. His students learned to sit very still for a long time, breathing slowly. They learned shadowboxing and hand movements. All these movements came to be called *kung fu.*

When a Japanese army invaded a Chinese island, kung fu experts came to the rescue. They turned back the spears of the Japanese with their bare hands. The amazed Japanese called this weapon *kara* (empty) *te* (hand). Some Japanese then learned karate themselves, keeping it a secret for centuries. But after World War II, American soldiers discovered karate. The secret was no longer a secret. Teachers opened schools for people wanting to learn this ancient art. Today, karate schools are all over the world.

1 **A monk came from India to —**

   A China.

   B Japan.

   C America.

   D an island.

   Hint: Look at the first sentence.

2 **Now karate schools are —**

   F for fighters.

   G in Japan.

   H for strong hands.

   J all over the world.

   Hint: Look at the last sentence in the second paragraph.

3 **How did Chinese kung fu experts turn back the Japanese?**

   _____

   _____

   _____

   _____

   _____

   _____

   _____

   _____

   Hint: Look at the second sentence in the second paragraph.

TEST TIP

When you have to provide a short answer, begin by restating the question. This strategy will help you make sure that your answer stays on target. For example, to answer question 3, you should begin by writing, "Chinese kung fu experts turned back the Japanese by . . ."

GO ON

Answers
1 Ⓐ Ⓑ Ⓒ Ⓓ   2 Ⓕ Ⓖ Ⓗ Ⓙ

Skill 2: Identifying Supporting Ideas

Sometimes it is helpful to arrange events in the order they happened. This may help you to understand the passage better.

The Mohawks once lived in Canada, but they grew weary of battling with the Algonquins there. So they moved south and settled on the banks of the Hudson River. Occasionally, however, some made short trips back to their old home. On one trip, enemies captured the Mohawk chief and his oldest son. The chief's wife and younger son grieved deeply. "I will find my father and brother and return with them," declared the boy. "Every night, Mother, build a fire on this cliff. The light will guide us home."

The woman built a fire every night. Years went by, and she continued to wait. Every night she sat by the fire in sorrow, and her tears tumbled down the cliff. Finally, one night, her younger son climbed the cliff, carrying the bones of his father and brother. He and his mother wept together. Then Manitou, the Great Spirit, sent lightning to carry them to his home in the sky. That same bolt of lightning transformed the woman's tears to crystal, and today her crystal tears still glisten on Diamond Rock.

1   **Which of these happened first in the story?**

A   The Mohawks moved south to the Hudson River.

B   A chief and his son traveled back to their old home.

C   Enemies captured the Mohawk chief and his son.

D   The chief's wife and younger son grieved.

Hint: Read the beginning to find what happened first.

2   **When did the younger son and his mother weep?**

F   before the son went in search of his father and brother

G   on a trip down the Hudson River

H   after the son returned with the bones of his father and brother

J   when the son built a fire on the cliff

Hint: Read sentences 4 and 5 in the second paragraph.

3   **When did the younger son leave home?**

_____

_____

_____

_____

_____

_____

_____

Hint: Read sentences 4 and 6 in the first paragraph.

GO ON

Answers
1 Ⓐ Ⓑ Ⓒ Ⓓ   **2** Ⓕ Ⓖ Ⓗ Ⓙ

SKILL 2: IDENTIFYING SUPPORTING IDEAS

Written directions tell the reader how to do something. To follow them means to do them in the same order in which they are given.

It seemed simple enough, so Peter did not know why his mother was making such a big deal out of it. The college coach had called and asked him to send him a copy of his football schedule and high school transcript. They were considering giving him an athletic scholarship.

Peter went to the guidance office and got a copy of the transcript and walked to the post office to mail it. When he got there, he realized he had left the football schedule at home, so he went home and got that. Back at the post office, he realized that he needed an envelope and also that he should make copies of each item so that he would have them to send to other colleges that might call. So he left the post office again and went to the stationery store to make copies and buy envelopes. Luckily, he met his friend Tom, so that he could borrow a dollar to make copies.

Carrying the growing number of items in hand, Peter went back to the post office and started to address the envelope. Where was it going? He knew the coach's name, but not his address. So he called his sister from the pay phone in the lobby and asked her to read the return address of the school from the envelope on the kitchen counter. Finally, he folded the transcript and schedule in thirds, put them in the envelope, put a stamp on it (after waiting in line to buy one), and put it in the out-of-town slot in the lobby. Big deal.

1   What was the first thing that Peter did?

A   got a copy of his high school transcript

B   got a copy of his football schedule

C   had copies of his transcript made

D   went to the guidance office and asked about what he needed

Hint: Read the start of the passage until you come to the answer.

2   Before he spoke with Tom, Peter had realized all but one of the following —

F   that he needed the football schedule.

G   that he needed an envelope.

H   that he needed to make copies.

J   that he needed the coach's address.

Hint: Make a list of what Tom realized before he met his friend.

3   What did Peter do after he made the copies?

_____

_____

_____

_____

_____

_____

_____

_____

Hint: Read the part when Peter makes copies.

GO ON ▶

Answers
1   Ⓐ Ⓑ Ⓒ Ⓓ   2   Ⓕ Ⓖ Ⓗ Ⓙ

SKILL 2: IDENTIFYING SUPPORTING IDEAS

The setting of a story lets the reader know when and where it is taking place.

It was a gray November day in 1963. A fishing boat rocked in the Atlantic Ocean off the southern coast of Iceland. Suddenly, a great black cloud burst from the water. Loud noises rumbled from the ocean, too. The ship's captain sent out a radio call. Something very unusual was happening!

During the next three hours, many scientists and reporters arrived at the scene. By now the cloud was 12,000 feet high. Huge explosions sent ash, dust, and hot rocks into the air. The watchers could see something just under the water's surface. A fiery island was growing in the Atlantic. It was caused by a volcano in the ocean.

1   **The fiery island started growing in the year —**

A   1993.

B   1936.

C   1963.

D   1863.

Hint: This asks about when the story takes place.

TEST TIP

Read dates and numbers very carefully. Test writers often try to trick students who read too quickly. Look at the answer choices for question 1. Notice that they have many of the same digits. Answer B is very close to the correct answer, but two digits have switched places. Read carefully to avoid choosing this kind of wrong answer.

2   **The fishing boat was off the coast of —**

F   Ireland.

G   Greenland.

H   Iceland.

J   November.

Hint: This asks about where the story takes place.

3   **During what season did the volcano erupt?**

_____

_____

_____

_____

_____

_____

_____

Hint: This asks about when the story takes place.

STOP

Answers
1 Ⓐ Ⓑ Ⓒ Ⓓ   2 Ⓕ Ⓖ Ⓗ Ⓙ

SKILL 3: SUMMARIZING MAIN IDEAS

The main idea is the overall meaning of a piece of writing. Often the main idea is written in the passage.

Allied soldiers in World War II were trapped at Dunkirk, France, and they could not escape because the shallow water kept rescue ships from landing. But hundreds of people in England took rowboats, tugs, and barges across the English Channel. For eight days, this odd navy carried soldiers from the beaches to the large ships. More than 300,000 soldiers were taken to safety.

1   What is the main idea of this passage?

    A Small ships are better than big ships.

    B Many soldiers were saved.

    C Soldiers were rescued from Dunkirk by the English.

    D The big ships could not get into shallow water.

Hint: What does the whole story talk about?

Sharks have a number of "tools" that help them find food. They have a keen sense of hearing and can smell blood from almost 2,000 yards away. They also have a special system of channels in their skin that helps them feel the vibrations of a struggling swimmer. We know that in clear water, sharks can see their prey from about fifty feet away.

2   What is the main idea of this selection?

    F Sharks hear well.

    G Sharks have poor vision.

    H Sharks sense food in a special way.

    J Sharks like struggling swimmers.

Hint: What does the entire passage talk about?

Every year, hungry deer do millions of dollars' worth of damage to young pine trees. But scientists in Washington have found a way to protect the trees using a substance called *selenium.* Selenium produces a bad smell when dissolved. A bit of this element is put in the ground near trees. Rain dissolves the selenium, and the tree absorbs it. The bad smell keeps the deer away until the tree is fully grown.

3   What is the main idea of this passage?

_____

_____

_____

_____

_____

_____

_____

Hint: What is most of the passage about?

Answers
1 Ⓐ Ⓑ Ⓒ Ⓓ   **2** Ⓕ Ⓖ Ⓗ Ⓙ

SKILL 3: SUMMARIZING MAIN IDEAS

Often the main idea is not given in the text. Sometimes the reader needs to figure it out by putting the facts together.

The spots on a fawn's coat let it hide in shady areas without being seen. The viceroy butterfly looks like the bad-tasting monarch, so birds avoid both. The hognose snake hisses when it fears another animal. When the opossum is attacked, it plays dead. Distressed turtles hide in their shells until they're sure it's safe to come out again.

1   The main idea of the passage is —

   A   each species has a unique way of preserving itself.

   B   some harmless animals look dangerous.

   C   spots and stripes can make animals less visible.

   D   birds don't like monarch butterflies.

Hint: What is the entire paragraph trying to suggest?

Alfred Nobel invented dynamite to help builders. But it was used for war, which made him feel very guilty. He was a rich man, so he set up a $9 million fund. Today the fund is used to reward people who have improved human life. Nobel prizes are awarded in six fields including peace, medicine, and chemistry.

2   What is the main idea implied in the passage?

   F   Nobel wanted to have a positive impact on society.

   G   Nobel was afraid of failure.

   H   Nobel wanted his invention used for more purposes.

   J   Nobel's invention proved useless for building purposes.

Hint: Read the entire paragraph to determine the main idea suggested.

One hundred viruses placed side by side would be no wider than a human hair. But these germs cause more than fifty diseases. Chicken pox, colds, and rabies are all caused by viruses. More than 21 million people have died from the flu caused by these tiny germs. Scientists are seeking ways to get rid of these tiny killers.

3   What is the main idea of this passage?

_____

_____

_____

_____

_____

_____

_____

Hint: What is suggested, but not stated, in the passage?

TEST TIP

Remember that eliminating incorrect answers is a great way to find the right one. Suppose you are solving question 2. Answer G is not supported by the text—it says nothing about Nobel's fear of failure. Answer H is too vague. Answer J is inaccurate and it focuses on a detail, not the main idea. Can you see why the remaining answer is reasonable and correct?

GO ON ➤

Answers
1 Ⓐ Ⓑ Ⓒ Ⓓ   **2** Ⓕ Ⓖ Ⓗ Ⓙ

SKILL 3: SUMMARIZING MAIN IDEAS

A summary contains the main idea of a passage. A summary is brief, yet it covers the main points.

Aluminum once was a very expensive metal. It cost more than $500 a pound. But in 1886, two scientists discovered a way to make the metal more cheaply. Two years later, another scientist refined the process even more. Then the price of the metal was less than 30¢ a pound. Today aluminum is so cheap that it is often thrown away.

1 What is the best summary of this passage?

  A Aluminum used to cost a lot of money.

  B The price of aluminum has lowered over the years.

  C Scientists have refined the process of making aluminum foil.

  D Aluminum is a strong metal.

Hint: Look for the statement that sums up the passage.

Product codes are the bars and numbers on a product label. The first numbers tell which company made the item. The last numbers identify the product and size. A laser reads the bars at the checkout. The computer finds the price for that product and prints the price on the cash register receipt. Store owners can change prices of items simply by changing the computer. The records stored in the computer also help stores to determine which items sell well.

2 What is this passage mostly about?

  F Product codes were developed to ensure customer safety.

  G A product code system is an efficient way of pricing goods.

  H A machine can read numbers and bars.

  J Numbers are assigned to companies.

Hint: Which statement best describes the passage as a whole?

Answers
1 Ⓐ Ⓑ Ⓒ Ⓓ   2 Ⓕ Ⓖ Ⓗ Ⓙ

In 1815, Mount Tambora in Indonesia blew its top. The huge blast cut 4,000 feet off its peak, and it killed 12,000 people. The dust from the explosion spread around the world. It blocked the sunlight. Europe and America were very cold the following year. In June, ten inches of snow fell in New England. The year 1816 was called the year without any summer.

3   What is this story mostly about?

A Many people died because of Mount Tambora.

B A volcanic explosion in 1815 had a major impact.

C People gave an unusual name to the year 1816.

D Ten inches of snow fell in New England in June.

Hint: You need to read the entire passage to determine the best summary.

Air plants, such as mosses and lichens, grow on buildings and stones and get their food and water from the air around them. Plants that grow on trees, such as mistletoe, get their food and water from the trees they live on. Sometimes, the trees die if the plants growing on them take away too much food or water.

4   What is this story mostly about?

F Some kinds of plants grow on buildings.

G Mistletoe sometimes kills trees.

H Some plants don't have to live in soil to survive.

J Mosses and lichens get food and water in various ways.

Hint: Pick the choice that best covers the main point of the passage.

TEST TIP

When looking for a *main idea*, try to find a statement that tells about the entire passage, not just one detail. The best answer makes a generalization that applies to the whole passage.

For example, the passage for question 4 describes plants that grow on buildings and stones as well as plants that grow on trees. Look for an answer choice that tells the main point about both of these subjects.

SKILL 4: PERCEIVING RELATIONSHIPS AND RECOGNIZING OUTCOMES

Often when we read, we need to see cause-and-effect relationships. Knowing what happened and what made it happen will help us to better understand what we read.

Rodney bragged to his friends that he could find his way around anywhere. One day, though, Rodney was delivering pizza in a strange part of town. Though he searched for half an hour, he could not locate the address he needed. Finally, he had to stop to ask for directions. His face turned red, and he began to stutter as he asked how to find the place.

1   What happened when Rodney got embarrassed?

   A   He got overheated.

   B   He got lost.

   C   His face got red and he stuttered.

   D   He started bragging.

   Hint: Getting embarrassed is the cause. What happened as a result of this?

Over the years Jason and his dog, Flash, had shared many good times and great adventures. They played together, and sometimes they even slept together. But Flash got old, and his eyesight and hearing began to fade. He even started snapping at children, so Jason knew the time had come to put Flash to sleep. Although the idea of taking Flash to the vet made Jason very sad, he knew it was for the best.

2   What made Jason know the time had come to put Flash to sleep?

   F   Jason loved his dog Flash.

   G   Jason knew the vet needed business.

   H   Flash began to snap at children.

   J   Jason was very sad.

   Hint: Knowing the time had come to put Flash to sleep is the effect. What made this happen?

Angela did not like to go to the park any more. She used to spend her springtime afternoons there, enjoying the flowers and the fresh air. But now she saw more and more old people in the park, sitting alone on the benches. They seemed so sad and lonely that Angela wished she never had to grow old.

3   What caused Angela to dislike going to the park?

   A   Her fear that she would become allergic to the flowers.

   B   Seeing too many lonely old people.

   C   She was afraid that she might be robbed.

   D   The change of seasons made it less comfortable.

   Hint: Not going to the park is the effect. Pick the choice that made this happen.

The young man wouldn't listen to anyone. He was too sure of himself and felt he could handle any situation. Others had warned him not to camp alone in the freezing weather, but he did not listen to them. When he fell into icy water, he could not build a fire to warm himself. No one was there to help him.

4   What caused the young man to get into trouble?

   _____

   _____

   _____

   _____

   _____

   _____

   Hint: Getting into trouble is the effect. What made this happen?

GO ON ➡

Answers
1 Ⓐ Ⓑ Ⓒ Ⓓ   2 Ⓕ Ⓖ Ⓗ Ⓙ   3 Ⓐ Ⓑ Ⓒ Ⓓ

24

Skill 4: Perceiving Relationships and Recognizing Outcomes

Often, the reader can predict, or tell in advance, what is probably going to happen next. The reader must think about what would make sense if the story were to continue.

High school had not been an easy time for Diane. Her friends seemed to have so much more time for fun than she did. That just made today even more special. As she walked up the steps in her black cap and gown, she felt a real sense of pride. Glancing over at her parents, she saw her mother wipe a tear from her cheek.

1   What will probably happen next?

    A Diane will go to the library to study.

    B Diane will receive her diploma.

    C The family will go to dinner together.

    D Diane will give her mother a handkerchief.

Hint: Once you figure out what Diane is doing, you will know the answer.

May's parents were having guests for dinner. Her mother asked May to help set the table. She noticed that May was trying to carry too many dishes at one time. May loaded down a tray with ten crystal glasses and had trouble lifting the heavy tray. Her mother had warned her, but May paid no attention.

2   What will May probably do next?

    F drop the tray

    G set the table

    H serve the guests

    J stop listening to her mother

Hint: Think about what the passage seems to be leading toward.

It was Jonathan's first day at his new school. Before school, groups of students gathered in front of the building. It seemed as if everyone but Jonathan was with a group of friends. They were all talking and laughing together. He walked over to a bench and sat down to read. Then he noticed someone coming toward him. It was Paul, a boy he had met last summer at the local pool.

3   What will Jonathan probably do next?

    A get up and leave

    B go over to the group of students

    C say hello to Paul as he comes closer

    D ask Paul if he wants to go to the pool with him again

Hint: Based on the other sentences, what seems most likely to happen next?

To Sheila, the alarm clock seemed to go off especially early that morning. She forced herself out of bed and put on her running clothes. Once she was outside, the cold air helped her wake up. It was just a few days before the race, and she wanted to be in top condition.

4   What will Sheila probably do next?

_____

_____

_____

_____

_____

_____

_____

_____

Hint: You need to look at all the facts in the story. What is most likely to happen next?

STOP

Answers
1 Ⓐ Ⓑ © Ⓓ   **2** Ⓕ Ⓖ Ⓗ Ⓙ   **3** Ⓐ Ⓑ © Ⓓ

Often texts come with graphs or diagrams. They help the reader understand the passage better.

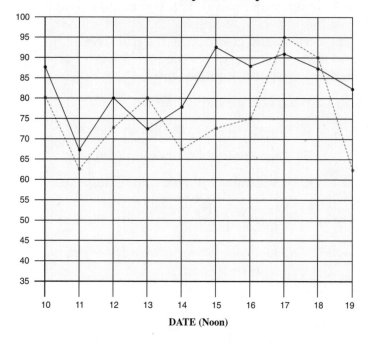

Temperature and Humidity for Ten Days in May

KEY

———— Temperature in Degrees

------------ Humidity in Percent

The weather in Florida varies somewhat, but it always seems that there is a lot of humidity in May. Both the temperature and humidity vary considerably. Low humidity with warm temperatures is the perfect type of weather for the beach. The discomfort and perspiration index seem to rise as the humidity rises.

1 On which day did both the humidity and temperature drop about twenty percent?

A   May 11

B   May 13

C   May 15

D   May 16

Hint: Check the "Temperature" and "Humidity" lines for each of the dates in the choices.

2 According to the graph, which would be the worst beach day? Why?

_____

_____

_____

_____

_____

_____

_____

Hint: First decide what would make up the worst beach day, according to the author.

GO ON ⇒

Answers

1 Ⓐ Ⓑ Ⓒ Ⓓ

John F. Kennedy High School's Best Race Times

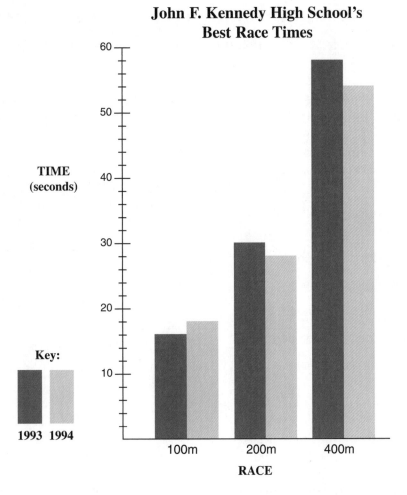

TIME (seconds)

Key:

1993 1994

RACE

John F. Kennedy High School's track team has won its second 200m race championship. It finished both the 100m and 400m in second place. Although Kennedy has a good team, Wedgewood High School had an outstanding year. They edged Kennedy in both the 100m and 400m but were not able to beat them in the 200m.

3 In the 1994 championship 200m race, the time it took Wedgewood High to run the race could have been —

F 32 seconds.

G 28 seconds.

H 26 seconds.

J 24 seconds.

Hint: Look at the bars on the graph that show Kennedy High's 200m time.

4 In which race did the Kennedy High team's performance get worse from 1993 to 1994?

_____

_____

_____

_____

_____

_____

_____

Hint: Read both the graph and the key that accompanies it.

GO ON

Answers
3 Ⓕ Ⓖ Ⓗ Ⓙ

SKILL 5: MAKING INFERENCES AND GENERALIZATIONS

When a reader makes an inference, it means that the information in the passage has told the reader something indirectly.

El Santo was a famous fellow in Mexico. He was successful as a wrestler, but he was also a top movie star. In his movies, he played a masked wrestler who helped catch criminals and monsters. His best film was *The Mummies of Guanajuato*. El Santo died in 1984.

1   What conclusion can you draw after reading this passage?

   A   The wrestler performed good deeds.

   B   El Santo hated wrestling.

   C   The Mexican people like wrestling.

   D   El Santo died at the hands of a criminal.

Hint: First eliminate the choices that you think cannot be right.

When people began to grow crops, they needed to know when to plant their seeds. They noticed that the best time to plant came at the same time each year. The early Egyptians counted the number of full moons between planting times. The times between moons were called months of the year. The Egyptians then noticed a bright star in the sky at planting time. They counted 365 days between the appearances of this star. Then they divided these days by 12 months to invent the first year.

2   What can you conclude after reading this?

   F   Egyptians invented the first calendar.

   G   The Egyptians invented time.

   H   The Egyptians were astronomers.

   J   The Egyptians counted one day every time the star appeared.

Hint: Although never stated, the selection is describing the invention of something.

The ancient Greeks made up stories to explain their world. They thought that many gods and goddesses controlled the universe. The greatest Greek god was Zeus, who controlled the weather. When a storm raged with thunder and lightning, Zeus was at work. The Greeks believed that the natural world was alive and that it should be treated with respect.

3   What is inferred by this passage?

   A   The Greeks did not understand science.

   B   The Greeks thought Zeus controlled the universe.

   C   The ancient Greeks weren't smart.

   D   The Greeks thought Zeus was the least powerful god.

Hint: Look for the choice that is not written in the passage, but implied.

Charlene awoke with a shriek. Her pajamas were soaked with sweat, and she could feel herself trembling. The night was dark and still, and the furniture in her room loomed like shadowy monsters. Charlene closed her eyes and tried to fall asleep again. But the night was too quiet, and her eyes popped open. Suddenly, Charlene heard a scratching noise at her window. She buried her head under her pillow, wishing the night was over.

4   What can you infer after reading this?

_____

_____

_____

_____

_____

_____

_____

Hint: Think about this happening to you.

GO ON ➡

Answers

1 Ⓐ Ⓑ Ⓒ Ⓓ   2 Ⓕ Ⓖ Ⓗ Ⓙ   3 Ⓐ Ⓑ Ⓒ Ⓓ

SKILL 5: MAKING INFERENCES AND GENERALIZATIONS

Sometimes a reader needs to generalize. This means to come up with a general statement about something in the text.

The special material in our body that makes us who we are is called DNA. Except for identical twins, everybody has different DNA. Since DNA is everywhere in the body, scientists believe that DNA patterns are better than fingerprints for identifying people.

1   From this story you can make the generalization that —

A DNA may become a commonly used way of identifying people.

B identical twins have the same fingerprints.

C fingerprints are the best way for the police to fight crime.

D DNA patterns for identical twins are similar.

Hint: Read the whole paragraph. Generalize what might happen in the future.

A comet is like a dirty ball of snow. It is made of frozen gases, frozen water, and dust. As a comet approaches the sun, the icy center gets hot and evaporates. The gases made by the evaporation form the tail of the comet. The dust left behind in the process forms meteor showers.

2   From this paragraph you can guess that —

F comets are made of snow.

G throwing a ball of snow can turn it into a comet.

H without the sun, a comet would look different to us.

J meteor showers are visible with a telescope.

Hint: Which choice is the best "guess"?

Nations fight wars for many reasons. In the 1880s, a war between the United States and Great Britain almost started because of a pig. The trouble took place on an island off the coast of Washington state. An American shot a pig owned by a British man. Tempers flared, and troops were sent to the island. The dispute, known as the Pig War, was soon settled without any fighting.

3   The story suggests that —

A many soldiers were injured in the war.

B the war was fought in Europe.

C the pig was cooked when the war ended.

D in the 1880s, the Americans and British did not get along well.

Hint: Which choice is a general statement rather than a specific one?

Mongooses are small Asian mammals that kill poisonous snakes and, sometimes, rats. In the 1890s, sugar planters in Hawaii imported mongooses to control the rats there. But the planters made a big mistake. They learned too late that mongooses roam by day, while rats roam by night. Now mongooses are a problem in Hawaii.

4   How did the sugar planters make their problems worse?

_____

_____

_____

_____

_____

_____

_____

Hint: What is the general idea of this passage?

GO ON

Answers

1 Ⓐ Ⓑ Ⓒ Ⓓ   2 Ⓕ Ⓖ Ⓗ Ⓙ   3 Ⓐ Ⓑ Ⓒ Ⓓ

A good reader will evaluate what he or she reads and make his or her own judgment about the text. Often things are implied in a text, rather than stated directly.

Tom Evans was on a field trip in Big Bend National Park in Texas. He and his college classmates had come from Chicago to hunt for fossils. As he was searching, Evans spotted something sticking out of a dirt mound. It turned out to be a major discovery. Evans had found the complete skull of a dinosaur. The four-foot-long skull came from a chasmosaurus, which resembled a rhinoceros. The skull had been buried for about eighty million years.

1   **What does this passage tell you about Tom Evans?**

   A   He was a straight-A student.

   B   He flew from Chicago to Big Bend National Park.

   C   He was an observant person.

   D   He enjoyed gardening.

   Hint: Review the facts. Think about what they say about Tom.

Longfellow wrote a poem that made Paul Revere famous for his ride to Concord to warn people that the British were coming. Actually, Revere never made it to Concord, nor was he alone. Two other riders, William Dawes and Dr. Samuel Prescott, went with him. It was Dr. Prescott who warned Concord about the British.

2   **From the paragraph, you can tell that —**

   F   the people of Concord weren't warned.

   G   Paul Revere had a friend named William Dawes.

   H   Longfellow was famous for his poetry.

   J   because of a well-known poem, people are misinformed about historical facts.

   Hint: You need to read the entire paragraph and evaluate the information before making a choice.

The Agriculture Department inspects packages from foreign countries. It makes sure that plant diseases aren't brought into the country. Dogs are trained to sniff for food. When the dogs smell food, they sit down by the passenger carrying it.

3   **From the passage, you can tell that —**

   A   the Agriculture Department provides us with an important safeguard.

   B   dogs bring a lot of disease into North America.

   C   it is not good to alert officials to food packages.

   D   food should be grown in North America and not imported.

   Hint: None of the choices are stated in the passage, but one of them is a conclusion that the reader can determine after reading the text.

When men sip drinks from cups, they usually look into them. Women usually look above the rim. Men often examine their nails with their palms facing upward and their fingers curled. But women extend their fingers with their palms facing downward to view their nails.

4   **What judgment can you make about men and women after reading this paragraph?**

   _____

   _____

   _____

   _____

   _____

   _____

   Hint: Read the entire paragraph. Think about the point that is being made.

GO ON

Answers
1 Ⓐ Ⓑ Ⓒ Ⓓ   2 Ⓕ Ⓖ Ⓗ Ⓙ   3 Ⓐ Ⓑ Ⓒ Ⓓ

SKILL 5: MAKING INFERENCES AND GENERALIZATIONS

The setting is the when and where of a story. The characters are the people or people-like figures in the story. The plot is the sequence of events that makes up the core of the story.

Ilse Bing was a photographer in the 1930s. She was one of the first photographers to use a camera to make works of art. Cameras had been around since the late 1800s. However, most photographers used them to take pictures of news events or famous people. Bing took photos of people who were dressed beautifully or oddly.

At about the same time, Laura Gilpin was working in the American Southwest. She took pictures as she hiked through the desert. One of Gilpin's most famous pictures is called "Shiprock, New Mexico." It shows a gigantic rock standing alone in a valley. Gilpin made many of her prints on a special soft paper. The special paper made her prints look cloudy and gray, like old paintings.

1   Ilse Bing was a photographer in the —

A   nineteenth century.

B   twentieth century.

C   eighteenth century.

D   twenty-first century.

Hint: Read the first sentence.

2   Laura Gilpin was working in —

F   the east.

G   the midwest.

H   the southwest.

J   the west.

Hint: Read the paragraph about Gilpin.

3   How were their photographs different?

_____

_____

_____

_____

_____

Hint: Read about both women's photos.

Louise and her mother were driving home one evening. They had been visiting Louise's aunt. Louise soon noticed that her mother was slowing down. It was getting impossible to see the road. For the next hour, their car crept slowly along the road. Headlights would suddenly appear in front of them, and they would move as far to the right of the road as they could. Both women were praying that they would get home safely.

4   What is the setting of this passage?

A   It was a bright night.

B   It was dark and foggy.

C   It was a poorly paved road.

D   There were large potholes in the road.

Hint: Picture the scene in your mind. Which choice seems most like that picture?

5   What conclusion can you draw about the characters' mood in this passage?

_____

_____

_____

_____

_____

_____

_____

Hint: Think about how you might feel in the same situation.

STOP

Answers

1 Ⓐ Ⓑ Ⓒ Ⓓ   2 Ⓕ Ⓖ Ⓗ Ⓙ   4 Ⓐ Ⓑ Ⓒ Ⓓ

31

SKILL 6: RECOGNIZING POINTS OF VIEW, FACTS, AND OPINIONS

The author's point of view is what he or she thinks or feels about what he or she is writing. Opinions express points of view.

The National Park System costs $1.2 billion annually to operate. Of that amount, $900,000 is spent on costs associated with visitors. The system has 368 locations, including major parks, such as the Grand Canyon, and small, specialized parks that feature one thing. We need to reexamine the type and quality of parks paid for by federal dollars. An independent commission could review the parks and determine whether or not they all should be kept open and what level of fees should be charged to park users. Currently, the people who use
parks pay less than ten percent of the costs of operating them.

1 What is the author suggesting?

   A A commission should start closing the smaller parks.

   B The government should pay a larger portion of the costs of running the national parks.

   C There is a need to reexamine the current parks to be sure we want to keep them and see if we need them all.

   D The National Park System will be fine if we just eliminate some of the smaller specialized parks.

   Hint: In this passage, the author's point of view is clearly stated in sentences 4 and 5.

2 The author would agree with which of the following?

   F The National Park System should continue as it is.

   G Government systems waste time and money.

   H It is good to reevaluate things as time goes on.

   J The park system should be shut down.

   Hint: Think about the author's point of view regarding the National Park System and figure out what he or she would most likely think about the choices given.

3 Should some national parks be closed because they are too expensive to run? Explain your answer.

   _____

   _____

   _____

   _____

   _____

   _____

   _____

   _____

   Hint: Use the information in the paragraph to form your opinion.

Answers

1 (A) (B) (C) (D)   2 (F) (G) (H) (J)

People are concerned that irradiated food will lead to an increase in cancer. But what about the benefits of reduced toxins, food decontamination, and a longer shelf life? Have x-rays caused people to become radioactive? Irradiation eliminates poisonous toxins and microorganisms. Scientists have found more of a chemical reaction in frozen and canned food than in food that has been irradiated. Sixty-seven percent of consumers would be willing to pay more for chicken that has significantly fewer toxins, according to a recent survey.

4 **With which statement would this author most likely agree?**

A Frozen foods are safer than irradiated foods.

B X-rays cause people to become radioactive.

C People are foolish to worry about cancer.

D Irradiation reduces the risks of contamination.

Hint: The answer is stated in the passage.

5 **What is the author's purpose in writing this selection?**

F to convince people that x-rays are unsafe

G to convince people that x-rays are safe

H to convince supermarkets to raise their prices

J to convince people that irradiated food is safe

Hint: Read the last sentence.

6 **List the benefits of irradiation that the author mentions in this paragraph.**

_____

_____

_____

_____

_____

_____

_____

Hint: Read the entire paragraph.

> ## TEST TIP
>
> Look for signal words that turn a statement into an opinion. An opinion often names something as the *best* or *worst* or claims that one thing is *better* or *worse* than another. Opinions also use words that make judgments, such as *foolish, clever, amazing, horrible,* or *ridiculous.*

GO ON

Answers
4 Ⓐ Ⓑ Ⓒ Ⓓ   **5** Ⓕ Ⓖ Ⓗ Ⓙ

When an author wants to convince the reader of something, he or she uses language that backs up his or her point of view. Often the language is very descriptive and emotional.

The money spent on political campaigns is paltry when compared to expenditures for commercial advertising. If we limited campaign spending, the incumbents would have an unfair advantage. Limiting campaign spending is like limiting free speech, which is embodied in the First Amendment of the Constitution. Maybe we should reform political campaigns, but not limit spending on them. What we really need to ensure is that all candidates who wish to can afford to campaign effectively.

1   The author is saying that —

   A   campaigns cost too much.

   B   campaign spending should not be limited.

   C   there should be an amendment to the Constitution.

   D   we should limit campaign spending.

   Hint: Read the entire paragraph.

2   When the author writes, "Limiting campaign spending is like limiting free speech," he is saying that —

   F   we should limit free speech.

   G   political campaigns should be free.

   H   since free speech is limited, we should limit campaign spending.

   J   limiting campaign spending is unconstitutional.

   Hint: Read the entire sentence.

National service can teach the values of hard work, self-sacrifice, and learning to live with different people. It can put our youth back to work. It can teach them job skills and instill the values of discipline, responsibility, and civic obligation. It can also provide long-term investment in the education and skills of our citizens. National service can also bring us together as a nation. We need to move back to a central core of beliefs.

3   What is the author promoting?

   A   making long-term investments

   B   writing a central core of beliefs

   C   living with different people

   D   starting a national service program

   Hint: Read the entire paragraph.

4   When the author writes, "It can also provide long-term investment in the education and skills of our citizens," she is trying to convince the reader that —

   F   the benefits of national service can last a lifetime.

   G   education is important to the citizens of this country.

   H   national service is a long-term program.

   J   education is more important than national service.

   Hint: Reread the sentence in context.

GO ON ▶

Answers

1 Ⓐ Ⓑ Ⓒ Ⓓ   2 Ⓕ Ⓖ Ⓗ Ⓙ   3 Ⓐ Ⓑ Ⓒ Ⓓ   4 Ⓕ Ⓖ Ⓗ Ⓙ

SKILL 6: RECOGNIZING POINTS OF VIEW, FACTS, AND OPINIONS

It is important to recognize the difference between fact and opinion. A fact is real and true. An opinion states a point of view. Words that describe are used to offer opinions.

Basketball is the only major sport that is a totally American game. Jim Naismith started it all. During the 1880s, Naismith taught athletics at a college in Massachusetts.

In the fall, Naismith's students spent long, exciting hours on the football field. But when winter came, the students moved indoors and did exercises. Most students soon grew bored. They kept asking for an indoor game that was as exciting as football.

Naismith began to think about a new kind of ball game that could be played safely in a small gym. He decided that players shouldn't use bats or run while holding the ball. Players would use only their hands to pass or throw the ball to other players. Naismith still had one big question. How would players score points? He went to the college store room and pulled out two peach baskets!

There was a balcony all around the gym. It was exactly ten feet above the floor. Naismith hung one peach basket on the balcony at each end of the gym. Then he divided the class into two teams of nine players each. The first basketball game began when he threw a soccer ball up between the team captains.

The players dashed up and down the gym, yelling with excitement as they tried to throw the ball into the peach baskets. The game stopped for a while when a player sank the ball. Someone climbed a ladder to get it out. After all, there is no hole in the bottom of a peach basket; but that was the only pause in the first basketball game. The final score was 1-0.

As basketball became popular at other colleges, teams made up their own rules. However, a set of rules was developed within a few years. A special ball and an open hoop took the place of the soccer ball and peach baskets. The game of basketball had begun.

1 **Which of the following is a fact about Jim Naismith?**

A He was a good teacher.

B He taught athletics.

C He preferred indoor sports to outdoor sports.

D Basketball players are overpaid because of him.

Hint: A fact is real and true. What is actually said in the story?

2 **Which of the following is a fact?**

F Basketball is as exciting as football.

G College basketball is more exciting than high school basketball.

H Basketball would be a better game if the baskets were lowered.

J The game of basketball has a set of rules.

Hint: Facts have to be true all the time. What is said in the story?

3 **Which of the following is NOT a fact from the story?**

A The balcony was ten feet above the gym floor.

B Each team had nine players.

C Basketball is the only major sport that is totally American.

D Naismith taught athletics at a college in the 1980s.

Hint: Three of the statements can be found in the story. One is not true.

GO ON

Answers
1 Ⓐ Ⓑ Ⓒ Ⓓ   **2** Ⓕ Ⓖ Ⓗ Ⓙ   **3** Ⓐ Ⓑ Ⓒ Ⓓ

Ending World Hunger

In some parts of the world, food shortages cause many people to starve. No one should have to be hungry. Somehow people must find a way to increase the world's food crop.

To do this, governments should grant more money to scientists who are studying little-known, edible plants. There are currently about 20,000 kinds of edible plants. Only about 100 of them are grown as food crops. People should take advantage of natural foods. It is unfair to allow people to starve while plants are available for them to eat.

A sensible solution to world hunger would be to direct government funds toward scientists. Spending money to end hunger in this way should be a goal for all governments.

4   **Which of the following is a fact from the selection?**

F   governments should grant money to scientists

G   there are about 20,000 kinds of edible plants

H   people should take advantage of natural foods

J   it is unfair to allow people to starve

Hint: Read the second paragraph

5   **The author's purpose in writing this selection is to—**

A   persuade people to eat more plants

B   describe the work of scientists

C   explain the causes of world hunger

D   propose a possible solution to food shortages

Hint: Read the last paragraph.

6   **What is the author's solution to world hunger?**

_____

_____

_____

_____

_____

_____

_____

Hint: Read the entire story.

TEST TIP

When you write a short answer, try to be as direct and clear as possible. After restating the question, provide a brief, precise answer. Do not worry if your answer seems obvious or easy, but take care to answer the question completely.

STOP

Answers
4 (F) (G) (H) (J)   5 (A) (B) (C) (D)

36

READING COMPREHENSION

Directions: Read the selection carefully. Darken the circle for the correct answer, or write your answer in the space provided.

| TRY THIS | More than one answer choice may sound correct. Choose the answer that goes best with the story. |

Sample A **Answering an Ad**

Josh had always wanted a pen pal. Therefore, he was excited to see the ad in his magazine guaranteeing to match people as pen pals. He followed the directions in the ad, and sent $5.00 and a brief letter describing himself to the address in the ad.

What did Josh hope to receive by following the directions in the ad?

A a pen

B $5.00

C a pen pal

D a magazine

| THINK IT THROUGH | The correct answer is <u>C</u>. Josh wanted a pen pal, and the second sentence states that the ad guaranteed to match pen pals. |

STOP

Adopting a Junior High School

Several schools in the southeastern part of our country were damaged or destroyed by a hurricane. These schools need help rebuilding in order to open by the beginning of October. The schools have asked for donations of school supplies.

Our school has adopted Jackson Junior High School in southern Florida. We will hold a school-supply drive to help the students of this school. The kinds of supplies needed include gym bags, locks for lockers, art boxes, scissors, pens and pencils, folders, and rulers. The school also needs books to help rebuild their school library.

The drive will begin on Monday, September 7 and end Friday, September 25. Please bring your donations to the school gym before or after school. Students wishing to volunteer to sort and pack items and label boxes, please contact the principal. I would like to take this opportunity to thank all donators and volunteers in advance for your support of this drive.

1 Why was a school-supply drive being held for Jackson Junior High School?

A The school had burned down.

B The school had hurricane damage.

C The students were very poor.

D Supplies were ruined by a flood.

2 Besides making donations, what else does the school want students to do?

_____

_____

_____

_____

_____

_____

GO ON

Answers
SA Ⓐ Ⓑ Ⓒ Ⓓ   1 Ⓐ Ⓑ Ⓒ Ⓓ

Hiking in a National Park

Emily pulled her jacket closer and looked into the campfire. The night was cold and clear, and even though it was too dark to see them, Emily could smell the pine trees that surrounded the campsite. Thousands of stars sparkled like tiny diamonds in the night sky. It was beautiful! Emily couldn't believe she was actually there in the national park. Just that morning when she woke up in her own bed she thought, "Another hot, humid, boring day, just like every other day this summer."

But then she remembered! Today was different. Her favorite aunt and uncle, Melissa and John, had invited her to join them on a backpacking trip. They had picked her up at 8:00 a.m. and had driven most of the day to get to the national park. They just had time to pitch their tents, build the fire, and cook dinner before it got dark. Emily had gone into the forest to gather firewood. Then she had helped Melissa make hamburger patties. She hadn't realized how hungry she was until she smelled them cooking. Everything tasted better when you were outside, she decided.

"Well, it's too dark to do anything else tonight," Uncle John said. "We might as well go to bed now so that we can get up at sunrise. I want to get an early start on the trail. Be sure to zip your tent, Emily. You wouldn't want to wake up with a rattlesnake in your sleeping bag!"

Emily couldn't decide whether he was teasing her or not. She made sure she zipped the tent tight, just in case. She crawled into her sleeping bag and wiggled around, trying to get comfortable. It had been a long day, but she was too excited to sleep. She wished she had brought a flashlight and a book. She wondered what adventures the next day would bring.

Emily woke up to the sounds of pots clanging. She crawled out of her tent and opened her backpack. "Look at this!" she exclaimed in dismay. Some small creature had chewed a hole in her bag of trail mix and eaten the whole thing. "Well, some little field mouse had a great breakfast!" Melissa said, "Never mind, I brought plenty of snacks for all of us."

After breakfast, Emily's uncle helped her adjust her backpack. It was heavier than she expected it to be. Then they took off on the trail. The three hikers followed a river for a while, then they crossed it.

Emily was *apprehensive*. She held her breath as she walked on the narrow log that served as a bridge. She didn't want to fall into the icy water.

The trail led back into the forest. Melissa walked in front, and Emily and John followed. Suddenly all three heard a terrifying sound—a loud, close rattle! Melissa jumped forward. Emily jumped backward and bumped into her uncle. About a foot to the right of the trail, they saw what was making the sound—a five-foot-long rattlesnake! The snake continued rattling its tail. They noticed something peculiar about the snake. Its mouth was wide open, and it was eating a field mouse. Apparently the snake was in the middle of its lunch.

John relaxed as soon as he realized what was happening. He explained that snakes' teeth point inward. It's very difficult for them to spit something out once they have begun eating. The rattlesnake couldn't harm them as long as it had something in its mouth. Melissa got her camera. They sat a short distance away and took pictures while they observed the rattlesnake. The snake continued to rattle but didn't move away. John told Emily that snakes eat only every ten days or so. It takes them a long time to swallow and digest their prey.

After a while, they left the snake and began hiking again. Emily's heart was still beating fast. She decided that Uncle John hadn't been teasing when he told her to zip up her tent. He wouldn't have to remind her about that tonight!

3 This selection is mainly about—

   F summer vacations.

   G the danger of rattlesnakes.

   H getting along with relatives.

   J hiking in a national park.

4 At the beginning of the selection Emily feels —

   A angry and disappointed.

   B worried and nervous.

   C excited and happy.

   D lonely and sad.

5 What is the last thing Emily did before she went to sleep?

   F She wiggled around, trying to get comfortable.

   G She zipped up the tent.

   H She helped Melissa make hamburger patties.

   J She went looking for rattlesnakes.

6 What did the snake most likely do after the three hikers left?

   _____

   _____

   _____

   _____

   _____

7 What happened to Emily's bag of trail mix?

   A Emily ate it.

   B Her Uncle John ate it.

   C It fell out of Emily's backpack.

   D A small animal ate it.

8 The word *apprehensive* means—

   F amused.

   G fearful.

   H excited.

   J careless.

9 Uncle John told the others that—

   A rattlesnakes have a good sense of smell.

   B rattlesnakes cannot hear.

   C snakes have teeth that point inward.

   D coyotes and foxes eat rattlesnakes.

10 What lesson did Emily learn by the second night?

   _____

   _____

   _____

   _____

> ## TEST TIP
>
> When the answer is not obvious, try rereading the passage. Circle clue words in the question to focus your search. For example, these clue words ask about the *sequence* or time order: *beginning, first, before, after, last, ending.*

GO ON

Answers

   3 Ⓕ Ⓖ Ⓗ Ⓙ   **5** Ⓕ Ⓖ Ⓗ Ⓙ   **8** Ⓕ Ⓖ Ⓗ Ⓙ

   4 Ⓐ Ⓑ Ⓒ Ⓓ   **7** Ⓐ Ⓑ Ⓒ Ⓓ   **9** Ⓐ Ⓑ Ⓒ Ⓓ

Notice for Eighth-Grade Students and Their Parents!

As you may know, all eighth-grade students are invited to participate in an outdoor education program. This program will once again be held at Fullersburg Outdoor Education Center, which is approximately 90 miles from our school.

Students will leave school the morning of the first day, travel by school bus to Fullersburg, sleep over three nights, and return the evening of the fourth day. All meals will be provided by the center. The school PTA has agreed to pay for the cost of room and board for each student. The school district will pay for the remaining costs, including the program and the bus transportation.

Participation in this program is open to all students who are able and willing to behave appropriately on an outing in which cooperation, respect for others, and following directions is expected. School behavior will be used to help determine the participants. Students who do not participate in the outdoor education program will attend classes at school.

All eighth-grade teachers and the principal will also attend the program as chaperons. The staff at Fullersburg will provide the instructional program.

Reservations for the trip must be made by completing the attached reservation form and returning it to the school by March 15.

The Fullersburg Outdoor Education Center

Fullersburg Outdoor Education Center contains several hundred acres of wooded land along the Salt River. There are a variety of trees, a swamp area, and a dry creek bed. During the Great Depression the Civilian Conservation Corps planted trees and built shelters throughout the center.

The heated lodge at the center was completed in 1981. The lodge consists of a large classroom, a kitchen, a glassed-in dining area with a breathtaking view of the woods and river, a nature museum, two bunk rooms with bathrooms, and private sleeping quarters for chaperons.

The daily schedule for students at Fullersburg includes breakfast and clean-up, an outdoor activity with an instructional follow-up, lunch and clean-up, an outdoor activity with an instructional follow-up, supper and clean-up. After supper there are recreational activities. Before bedtime there are treats, an evening program, and then showers.

Some of the outdoor activities that students can choose include archery, horseback riding, hiking, orienteering, animal tracking, bird watching, fishing, and canoeing. If there is enough snow on the ground, students may choose cross-country skiing, sledding, or snowshoeing as an activity. If the river is frozen, students may play broom hockey or ice skate.

GO ON

11 According to the flyer, the outdoor education program—

    F has never been held at Fullersburg before.

    G is usually held at the school.

    H has been held at Fullersburg in the past.

    J is held at different places each year.

12 According to the flyer, who is invited to participate in the outdoor education program?

    A all seventh- and eighth-grade students

    B eighth-grade students who are on the honor roll

    C eighth-grade students and their parents

    D all eighth-grade students who can behave properly

13 Costs for the outdoor education program will be paid for by—

    F the PTA and the school district.

    G the students.

    H the parents.

    J the teachers and community businesses.

14 Where would this notice most likely be found?

_____

_____

_____

_____

_____

_____

_____

15 According to the flyer, which of these statements is true?

    A Fullersburg is located several hundred miles from the school.

    B The students will need to provide their own transportation to the center.

    C Students who do not participate in the outdoor program will attend classes taught by the principal at the school.

    D The staff at Fullersburg will provide the instructional program.

16 Which of these statements is an *opinion* in the flyer?

    F The outdoor education center is located along the Salt River.

    G The heated lodge at the center was completed in 1981.

    H Students are expected to clean up after themselves.

    J The dining area has a breathtaking view of the woods and river.

17 According to the selection, the students can play broom hockey—

    A in the bunk rooms.

    B in the glassed-in dining room.

    C on the river if it is frozen.

    D in the large classroom.

18 What might be the author's purpose in writing this flyer?

_____

_____

_____

_____

_____

_____

_____

GO ON

Answers
11 Ⓕ Ⓖ Ⓗ Ⓙ   **13** Ⓕ Ⓖ Ⓗ Ⓙ   **16** Ⓕ Ⓖ Ⓗ Ⓙ
12 Ⓐ Ⓑ Ⓒ Ⓓ   **15** Ⓐ Ⓑ Ⓒ Ⓓ   **17** Ⓐ Ⓑ Ⓒ Ⓓ

41

The Sport of In-line Skating

Most people are familiar with roller-skating. In-line skating, however, is one of the fastest-growing sports in the world. In 1984 there were 20,000 in-line skaters. By 1992 there were more than three million in-line skaters.

In-line skates have a single row of polyurethane rollers attached to the bottom of a padded boot. The number of rollers on a skate can vary from three to five. At the rear of the skate is a heel stop.

I bought my first pair of in-line skates with money that I had saved from birthdays and from baby-sitting jobs. I bought a pair of four-wheeled skates for $65.00. I also decided to buy the safety equipment—gloves, helmet, kneepads, elbow pads, wrist guards—recommended by friends who are in-line skaters. I left the store broke, but *exhilarated*.

As soon as I got home I wanted to start skating. A friend who is a member of the International In-line Skating Association suggested that I learn to stop before I started to skate. She suggested that I practice on a safe grassy area. So I walked to a nearby park. I spent about an hour practicing to stop. When I felt comfortable stopping, I found an empty tennis court and I practiced skating strokes. I fell several times. Each time I fell, I was grateful that I was wearing the safety equipment. I'll never forget that day. My body was in pain, but my spirit was lifted by the thrill of gliding across cement.

It has been three years since I bought my first in-line skates. My friends and I belong to an in-line skating club. Our local YMCA allows us to use their rink, and the health club allows in-line skating an hour every day in the gym. I believe that my skills at in-line skating are good enough for me to become a professional skater.

GO ON ▶

19 In this selection, the word *exhilarated* means—

F exhausted.

G excited.

H excluded.

J expanded.

20 The selection implies that roller-skating is—

A as popular as in-line skating.

B more difficult than in-line skating.

C a sport of the past.

D not as safe as in-line skating.

21 What is at the rear of an in-line skate?

F a heel stop

G a polyurethane roller

H a safety guard

J a distance meter

22 Which of these is an *opinion* in the selection?

A In-line skating is one of the fastest-growing sports in the world.

B My skills at in-line skating are good enough for me to become a professional skater.

C In-line skates can have three, four, or five wheels.

D Safety equipment for in-line skating includes gloves, a helmet, kneepads, elbow pads, and wrist guards.

23 What should you do if you were asked to skim this selection?

F carefully reread the selection

G recall the main idea of the selection

H quickly look through the selection

J review your notes about the selection

24 The web shows some important ideas in the selection. Fill in the empty boxes with the missing information.

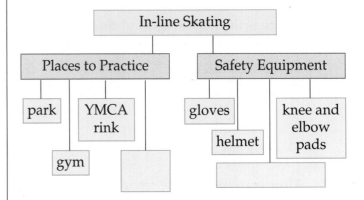

25 Describe the author's first day on in-line skates.

_____

_____

_____

_____

_____

_____

TEST TIP

Notice the clue word *first* in question 25. Your answer should not retell the entire story. It should focus on the *first* time the author tried in-line skates.

GO ON

Schedule for Jefferson County Fair				
FRI.	11:00–12:00	1:00	2:00	3:00
	Judging of 4-H craft projects	Footraces ————————————————————————→		
		Toddlers	4-, 5-year-olds	6-, 8-year-olds
SAT.	Pet parade	Footraces ————————————————————————→		
	Judging of 4-H farming projects	9-, 10-year-olds	11-, 12-year-olds	13-, 14-year-olds
			Teddy bear picnic	
SUN.	Baby contest	Crowning of 4-H king and queen	Marching band contest	
	Judging of 4-H livestock projects			

26 When is the marching band contest scheduled to take place?

   A Sunday at 11:00

   B Saturday at 2:00

   C Sunday at 2:00

   D Saturday at 11:00

27 How many events are scheduled for Sunday?

   F 2

   G 3

   H 4

   J 5

28 For a 4-H project, Kyle raised a pig named Rufus and entered it in the fair. When would Kyle learn if Rufus won a prize?

   _____

   _____

   _____

   _____

   _____

   _____

   _____

29 What event will be missed by the 11-, 12-year-olds who participate in the footraces?

   A Pet parade

   B Crowning of king and queen

   C Teddy bear picnic

   D Baby contest

30 If 11-year-old Carole and 12-year-old Rachel entered the footraces, when would their race take place?

   F Friday at 1:30

   G Friday at 3:00

   H Saturday at 1:30

   J Saturday at 2:00

31 Where would you most likely find this schedule?

   _____

   _____

   _____

   _____

   _____

   _____

   _____

STOP

A sample question helps you to understand the type of question you will be asked in the test that follows.

Sample A

Going Camping

Jen is very excited about going camping with her cousins Bill and Mindy. The cousins are good friends. The campers plan to travel to the Grand Canyon, where they will stay for two weeks.

On their trip the three cousins most likely will—

A be very bored

B fight and argue continually

C have an enjoyable time

D ignore one another

For questions 1–35 carefully read each selection and the questions that follow. Then darken the circle for the correct answer, or write your answer in the space provided.

Visiting a High-Altitude City

A visitor to a city in Bolivia such as La Paz might find the following recommendations in a brochure in the hotel room:

If it is your first day here in our lovely city, you must take it easy and rest. We recommend that you not walk for even short distances. You must not climb stairs.

These recommendations are posted in hotel rooms to help warn visitors of the potential hazards of being at a high altitude. You see, La Paz is located at a high altitude in the Andes Mountains. People who are not used to living at such altitudes can contract *sorojche,* or altitude sickness. Nausea, headaches, and tired muscles are some of the symptoms of this illness. These symptoms are caused by lack of oxygen from the thin air at high altitudes.

People who rent cars in La Paz are given containers of water to take with them. Car radiators quickly boil over in high altitudes, because water boils at a lower temperature in high altitudes than in low altitudes. Water needs to be replaced often in radiators of cars driven at high altitudes.

1 How do people get *sorojche*?

A by driving too fast

B from resting the day they arrive in a city

C by buying it in a local store

D from too much activity the first few days in a high-altitude location

2 This article was written mainly to—

F explain the hazards of a high altitude.

G describe things to see in La Paz.

H welcome visitors to Bolivia.

J help you take care of rental cars.

3 Why should people who rent cars take containers of water with them?

_____

_____

_____

_____

_____

_____

_____

GO ON

Answers

SA Ⓐ Ⓑ Ⓒ Ⓓ   **1** Ⓐ Ⓑ Ⓒ Ⓓ   **2** Ⓕ Ⓖ Ⓗ Ⓙ

VISIONEAR

The latest ALL-IN-ONE ENTERTAINMENT CENTER includes:

- 27-inch television
- DVD recorder and player
- speaker phone

- CD player
- fax machine
- color printer

- personal computer

Other features include: remote control, 195 TV channels, and a superior sound system.

• •

This Entertainment Center is the latest innovation in sight and sound. IT DOES EVERYTHING except pop your popcorn! You can actually cruise the Internet and talk to your friends on the speaker phone while you watch your favorite television program.

Many people already enjoy the convenience of *VISIONEAR*. You should be part of the "VISION" crowd and own one too! Imagine how people will look up to you because you were smart enough to be one of the FIRST people to own this superior Entertainment Center.

VISIONEAR is a quality product that everyone wants to own. We back this product with our 100% money-back guarantee, good for 40 days. NO IFS, ANDS, or BUTS. If you don't want it, we'll take it back. There is a small charge for restocking the product.

GO ON ➤

4 This ad suggests that the Visionear—

A has advanced technology.

B has a popcorn popper.

C is inexpensive to purchase.

D is too heavy for one person to carry.

5 This ad was written mainly to tell about—

F the company that produces Visionear.

G the uses of a fax machine.

H a new home entertainment center.

J the cheapest television set for sale.

6 Which of these is an *opinion* in the ad?

A Other features include: remote control...

B You can actually cruise the Internet...

C Visionear is a quality product...

D There is a small charge for...

7 If you were asked to rename the Visionear, what would you call it? Why?

_____

_____

_____

_____

_____

_____

8 The ad tries to appeal to your desire to—

F save the environment.

G be one of the first people to own the product.

H get good grades in school.

J travel to other countries and see new places.

9 There is enough information in this ad to show that Visionear—

A is a fairly new product.

B has been tested by a government agency.

C is not expensive.

D has an automatic shut-off system.

10 The Visionear has a money-back guarantee for—

F 30 days.

G 40 days.

H 90 days.

J 100 days.

11 What else would you like to add to the Visionear?

_____

_____

_____

_____

_____

_____

_____

GO ON

Answers

4 Ⓐ Ⓑ Ⓒ Ⓓ   6 Ⓐ Ⓑ Ⓒ Ⓓ   9 Ⓐ Ⓑ Ⓒ Ⓓ

5 Ⓕ Ⓖ Ⓗ Ⓙ   8 Ⓕ Ⓖ Ⓗ Ⓙ   10 Ⓕ Ⓖ Ⓗ Ⓙ

Sally Ride Makes History in Space

On June 18, 1983, Sally Ride became the first American woman to travel in space. She helped place three satellites over different parts of the world and conducted science experiments. But just as important as the scientific duties she performed, Ride showed a generation of girls that they could reach for the stars. The fields of science and space exploration were now open to women as well as men.

Sally Ride was born on May 26, 1951, in California. As a child her two favorite activities were sports and reading. She loved to play softball, football, and soccer. When she was about ten years old, she began to play tennis. She became one of the top junior tennis players in the country and was offered a tennis scholarship at a private high school in Los Angeles. It was there that she became truly interested in the field of science.

In college Sally Ride continued to play tennis and to study science. Her favorite subjects were astronomy and physics, and, after a few years, Sally also started taking English courses. She especially liked learning about Shakespeare. Sally Ride graduated from Stanford University in 1973 with degrees in English and physics. She continued graduate school at Stanford, combining her interests in physics and astronomy, and received a doctorate in *astrophysics.*

One day while Sally was looking for a job, she saw an advertisement from NASA (National Aeronautics and Space Administration) in the Stanford school paper. NASA was seeking applicants for a new space shuttle program. They were looking for engineers, scientists, and doctors to train as part of a group of astronauts, so Sally completed the forms and became one of the 208 finalists. The finalists were sent to the Johnson Space Center in Houston, Texas, where they were asked many questions. They were tested on how they would perform in an emergency situation. They also had to show that they were in good physical condition. Sally was thankful that she had always been physically active.

In January 1978, Sally Ride was selected to be one of the 35 astronaut candidates. The candidates moved to Houston for one year of training. If they successfully completed the training, they would have the opportunity to become astronauts. Sally's future husband, Steven Hawley, was also in this group. In 1979 both Ride and Hawley became astronauts.

In April 1982, Ride called her family and announced that she had been chosen as one of the astronauts for the seventh shuttle flight! The five astronauts worked closely together in a large office for the next year. They trained for the flight and learned to work together as a team.

On the day the space shuttle was to lift off, crowds of onlookers gathered along the Florida beaches to witness the launch. The mission went very smoothly and satellites were launched over Canada, Indonesia, and Germany. The flight lasted six days and made 98 orbits around the earth. When it touched down, Sally Ride had made history.

GO ON ➧

12 Sally Ride became famous as the first—

   A astronaut in space.

   B woman in space.

   C scientist in space.

   D American woman in space.

13 Which of the following is an *opinion*?

   F Sally Ride liked playing sports.

   G Sally Ride became a valuable role model for girls.

   H Sally Ride studied science in college.

   J Sally Ride graduated from Stanford University in 1973.

14 In this selection the word *astrophysics* means—

   A the study of marketing and advertising.

   B the study of the way people lived in the past.

   C the study of the physical and chemical nature of stars.

   D the study of the human mind.

15 What was the first step Sally Ride took in becoming the first American woman to travel in space?

_____

_____

_____

_____

_____

_____

16 This article would most likely be found in a book titled—

   F *Famous Soccer Players.*

   G *People Who Love Shakespeare.*

   H *American Women in Space.*

   J *Scientific Experiments in Space.*

17 How did Sally Ride's love of sports help her become an astronaut?

   A Astronauts should play tennis well if they want to be successful.

   B Participating in sports kept her in top physical condition.

   C Only people who are very coordinated can become astronauts.

   D All astronauts love sports.

18 Why did the five astronauts who were chosen for the seventh shuttle flight work together in one large office?

   F NASA wanted all of the astronauts in the same room for security reasons.

   G They needed to learn to work together.

   H NASA didn't have much office space.

   J They were all good friends and did not want separate offices.

19 If the author added a paragraph at the end of this selection, what would it include?

_____

_____

_____

_____

_____

_____

_____

GO ON

Suffering from Allergies

Do you suffer from allergies? Did you know that more than forty million people in the United States have allergy problems? You may have heard the word *allergy* many times without knowing exactly what it means. An allergy is an unusual reaction to something that is harmless to most people. For example, if you have a ragweed allergy, you probably start sneezing whenever you are near ragweed. If you have a shellfish allergy, you might develop a rash if you eat lobster, shrimp, or crayfish.

People have probably had allergies throughout history. The paintings on the wall of an Egyptian ruler's tomb show that he died after being stung by a bee. This was a violent allergic reaction! Around A.D. 200 a Greek physician wrote about people sneezing when they were exposed to certain plants. Although allergies have existed for thousands of years, it was not until the mid-1800s that the medical community began to understand the causes and characteristics of allergies. At that time an English physician, W. R. Kirkman, collected the yellow dust called pollen from grasses he had grown. When he began to sneeze, he realized that he had discovered the cause of hay fever.

About the same time, another English doctor, Charles Blackley, developed an allergy test. He scratched one of his arms and put rye grass pollen on the cut. The scratch itched, swelled, and turned red. Blackley then scratched his other arm without adding pollen to the cut. Nothing happened. Blackley had the proof that he was allergic to rye grass. This test is called a scratch test, and it is still used today.

Our bodies protect us from germs and viruses by making substances called *antibodies*. Antibodies fight the germs and viruses that cause illness. An allergic reaction is really a mistake—the body mistakes something that is usually harmless, such as pollen, for a harmful invader. Special antibodies are produced and then the body releases a chemical that causes a runny nose, itchy skin, and sometimes, wheezing.

The material that produces an allergic reaction is called an allergen. Many allergens, such as mold, pollen, and mites, are present in the air. Mold is a small plant that grows in wet places. Mold spores are carried by the wind. Many grasses, weeds, and trees produce pollen that is carried by the wind. Mites are insects that are so small they cannot be seen. If you sneeze when the wind blows, you may be allergic to one of these things.

People can be allergic to many different things. Some people are allergic to certain foods. Their allergic reactions to these foods often include upset stomach, rashes, or breathing problems. Some foods that can cause allergic reactions are dairy products, wheat, corn, nuts, seafood, eggs, chocolate, and oranges.

Some people are allergic to drugs such as aspirin and penicillin, and other people are allergic to certain chemicals present in soaps and paints. Some people have allergic reactions when they are stung by bees or bitten by ants or mosquitoes. Doctors can help the allergy sufferer by prescribing pills, sprays, or nose drops. If these don't provide relief, doctors sometimes suggest allergy shots.

GO ON

20 This selection would *most* likely be found in—

A a travel guide to Greece.

B an economics textbook.

C a health magazine.

D a world history textbook.

21 In an allergic reaction, the body mistakes an allergen for—

F pollen.

G an antibody.

H a blood cell.

J a harmful invader.

22 The third paragraph tells about—

A the history of allergies.

B the causes of allergies.

C the development of the scratch test.

D how to avoid allergies.

23 In the fourth paragraph, the word *antibodies* means—

F germs blown in the wind.

G viruses that attack the body.

H substances the body makes to fight illness.

J medicine given to allergy sufferers.

24 How do we know that people had allergies thousands of years ago?

_____

_____

_____

_____

_____

_____

25 All of the following phrases describe mold *except*—

A it grows in wet places.

B it protects us from viruses.

C it is a small plant.

D its spores are carried by the wind.

26 If you have hay fever, you will probably—

F avoid fields when grasses are producing pollen.

G use special soap to avoid getting a rash.

H produce allergens.

J avoid eating any dairy products.

27 If you sneeze when the wind blows you may be allergic to—

A aspirin and penicillin.

B mold, pollen, or mites.

C chocolate or shellfish.

D ants and bees.

28 Why do you think the author wrote this article?

_____

_____

_____

_____

_____

_____

_____

GO ON ⟹

A Visit to the Rain Forest

"I can't believe that you and I are both winners in the Amazon Rain Forest Adventure!" shouted Jess to her friend and fellow environmentalist.

"It is highly unusual for the government to choose two students from the same school for this educational journey. But we both worked hard on our science experiments, and our essays about why we wanted to go on this trip were chosen first and second in the state. Also, Mr. Hancock recommended both of us to the selection committee," Winnie responded with enthusiasm.

Jess and Winnie were both members of the school's Environmental Impact Committee (EIC). They made posters explaining the importance of the rain forests and how they provide Earth with forty percent of its oxygen supply by converting carbon dioxide into oxygen. Jess and Winnie also contacted speakers from the local university. These speakers conducted a school assembly showing the kinds of animals and plants that live in the rain forests and are in danger of becoming *extinct* as the rain forests disappear.

The girls' two-week trip to Brazil's Amazon Rain Forest started in Macapá, a city located at the mouth of the Amazon River. There were eight other students in their group. Four adults guided the students on a boat trip down the Amazon. During their journey they saw piranha (fish with razor-sharp teeth), alligators, monkeys, passion-fruit trees, and gorgeous flowers in every color imaginable. When the group reached Manaus they made themselves comfortable in a cabin near the river.

"The first night in the cabin was the most unforgettable. All night long I could hear the cries of animals in the rain forest, but of course I could see nothing because there were no lights near our cabin. I was nervous and afraid to sleep," said Winnie in her talk with her peers upon returning home from Brazil.

"I was so tired that first night from the exhaustion of canoeing for six hours that I slept very well," explained Jess.

"I was impressed with the difficult life of the people who live in the rain forest. They have none of the conveniences that we take for granted. They love the environment, though, and do not abuse it. I think this is partly because they are very dependent on their environment for the things they need to live," said Winnie.

"While I was in the rain forest enjoying its beauty and unique ecosystem, I thought about what I could do to help save this special place," said Jess. "I've decided to design a reusable container for use in grocery stores instead of grocery bags. This will lessen the number of trees cut down to make the bags. I hope to sell the bags to consumers and use the profits to buy as many acres of rain forest as possible," explained Jess.

GO ON

29 The description of the trip along the Amazon River helps you understand—

F the work done by the university researchers.

G the environment of a rain forest.

H the enthusiasm the girls felt for their trip.

J the rain forest at night.

30 In this selection, the word *extinct* means—

A no longer existing.

B no longer active.

C no longer burning.

D no longer being used.

31 The device the author uses in the first two paragraphs is—

F suspense.

G dialogue.

H repetition.

J flashback.

32 This selection would most likely be found in a book titled—

A *Science Experiments.*

B *School Assembly.*

C *Educational Adventures.*

D *The History of Recycling.*

TEST TIP

Question 32 is similar to a main idea question. Decide which of these titles includes the main idea of the article.

33 Winnie explained why she was afraid the first night in the cabin so that—

F her fellow students would understand how she felt.

G Jess would admit that she too was afraid at night.

H people would know why she did not like her trip.

J her friends would be afraid to visit the rain forest.

34 Toward the end of the selection, how does Winnie feel about the people of the rain forest?

_____

_____

_____

_____

_____

_____

_____

35 What does Jess decide to do to save the rain forest?

_____

_____

_____

_____

_____

_____

_____

STOP

UNIT 4
READING VOCABULARY

Directions: Darken the circle for the word or group of words that has the same or almost the same meaning as the underlined word.

TRY THIS — Choose your answer carefully. The other choices may seem correct. Be sure to think about the meaning of the underlined word.

Sample A

To <u>link</u> means to—

A separate   C clap

B join   D wash

THINK IT THROUGH — The correct answer is **B**, join. <u>Link</u> means "join." Link does not mean separate, clap, or wash.

STOP

1 To <u>amend</u> something is to—

  A repeat it   C correct it

  B copy it   D save it

2 To <u>meddle</u> is to—

  F ignore   H knit

  G interfere   J avoid

3 <u>Permanent</u> means—

  A lasting   C pleasant

  B annoying   D temporary

4 Something that is <u>witty</u> is—

  F foolish   H boring

  G serious   J clever

5 To <u>infuriate</u> is to make very—

  A frightened   C safe

  B happy   D angry

6 To <u>comply</u> is to—

  F obey   H pretend

  G suspect   J admire

7 An <u>intermission</u> is a kind of—

  A pamphlet   C recess

  B errand   D competition

8 A <u>hoax</u> is a kind of—

  F box   H trick

  G candy   J rope

9 To <u>cite</u> is to—

  A look over   C speak for

  B find out   D refer to

10 Something that is <u>profound</u> is—

  F deep   H easy

  G stupid   J shallow

STOP

Answers

SA Ⓐ Ⓑ Ⓒ Ⓓ   3 Ⓐ Ⓑ Ⓒ Ⓓ   6 Ⓕ Ⓖ Ⓗ Ⓙ   9 Ⓐ Ⓑ Ⓒ Ⓓ
1 Ⓐ Ⓑ Ⓒ Ⓓ   4 Ⓕ Ⓖ Ⓗ Ⓙ   7 Ⓐ Ⓑ Ⓒ Ⓓ   10 Ⓕ Ⓖ Ⓗ Ⓙ
2 Ⓕ Ⓖ Ⓗ Ⓙ   5 Ⓐ Ⓑ Ⓒ Ⓓ   8 Ⓕ Ⓖ Ⓗ Ⓙ

Directions: Darken the circle for the sentence that uses the underlined word in the same way as the sentence in the box.

| TRY THIS | Read the sentence in the box. Decide what the underlined word means. Then find the answer choice in which the underlined word has the same meaning. |

Sample A

> We made a <u>fast</u> exit from the crowded gym.

In which sentence does <u>fast</u> have the same meaning as it does in the sentence above?

A   The <u>fast</u> current washed the pier away.

B   The clock in the hall is running <u>fast</u>.

C   The baby was <u>fast</u> asleep in a crib.

D   You must <u>fast</u> before medical tests.

| THINK IT THROUGH | The correct answer is <u>A</u>. In choice <u>A</u> and in the sentence in the box, <u>fast</u> means "moving quickly." |

1

> Our team won first <u>place</u> in the race.

In which sentence does <u>place</u> have the same meaning as it does in the sentence above?

A   <u>Place</u> the bowl carefully on the table.

B   The beach is a quiet <u>place</u> to relax.

C   Which <u>place</u> at the table is yours?

D   Don't worry if you finish in last <u>place</u>.

2

> The actor forgot his opening <u>line</u>.

In which sentence does <u>line</u> have the same meaning as it does in the sentence above?

F   Don't cross the yellow <u>line</u> on a highway.

G   We had to stand in <u>line</u> to get movie tickets.

H   Can you rewrite the last <u>line</u>?

J   The children will <u>line</u> up to go outside.

3

> We'll all do our <u>part</u> on the project.

In which sentence does <u>part</u> have the same meaning as it does in the sentence above?

A   Which <u>part</u> of the city is the oldest?

B   Ben wants a <u>part</u> in the school play.

C   I replaced a broken <u>part</u> on my car.

D   Isabel won't <u>part</u> with her hat.

4

> Small <u>craft</u> are in danger in storms.

In which sentence does <u>craft</u> have the same meaning as it does in the sentence above?

F   The cat showed great <u>craft</u> in catching the mouse.

G   Sam can <u>craft</u> many things from wood.

H   Sailing <u>craft</u> of all types filled the harbor.

J   Weaving is an ancient <u>craft</u>.

Answers
SA ⒶⒷⒸⒹ   1 ⒶⒷⒸⒹ   2 ⒻⒼⒽⒿ   3 ⒶⒷⒸⒹ   4 ⒻⒼⒽⒿ

Directions: Darken the circle for the word or words that give the meaning of the underlined word, or write your answer in the space provided.

TRY THIS Read the first sentence carefully. Look for clue words in the sentence. Then use each answer choice in place of the underlined word. Be sure that your answer and the underlined word have the same meaning.

Sample A

The <u>dismal</u> weather has been cold and rainy for days. <u>Dismal</u> means—

A bright   C windy

B gloomy   D changeable

THINK IT THROUGH The correct answer is <u>B</u>. Dismal means "gloomy." The clue words are "cold" and "rainy." All four choices have something to do with weather. But only <u>gloomy</u> has the same meaning as <u>dismal</u>.

STOP

1 Miriam was <u>dubious</u> about her chances of winning. <u>Dubious</u> means—

A positive   C doubtful

B hopeful   D happy

2 The <u>sapling</u> had to be watered twice a day. A <u>sapling</u> is a—

F large bush   H species of tropical bird

G young tree   J type of rose

3 The stream <u>receded</u> after the rains stopped. <u>Receded</u> means—

A withdrew   C overflowed

B flowed   D flooded

4 The baby sitter tried to quiet the <u>boisterous</u> children. <u>Boisterous</u> means—

_____

_____

_____

_____

5 The student included many details and gave an <u>accurate</u> summary of the story. <u>Accurate</u> means—

F exaggerated   H poor

G exact   J partial

6 Painting is a <u>tedious</u> task because you must work slowly and carefully. <u>Tedious</u> means—

A painful   C boring

B creative   D interesting

7 The patient suffered <u>acute</u> pain from his injuries. <u>Acute</u> means—

F frequent   H intense

G slight   J mild

8 The charity had a fund-raiser to <u>generate</u> money for its projects. <u>Generate</u> means—

_____

_____

_____

_____

STOP

Answers
SA Ⓐ Ⓑ Ⓒ Ⓓ   2 Ⓕ Ⓖ Ⓗ Ⓙ   5 Ⓕ Ⓖ Ⓗ Ⓙ   7 Ⓕ Ⓖ Ⓗ Ⓙ
1 Ⓐ Ⓑ Ⓒ Ⓓ   4 Ⓐ Ⓑ Ⓒ Ⓓ   6 Ⓐ Ⓑ Ⓒ Ⓓ

Sample A

To <u>motivate</u> is to—

A discourage

B work

C accept

D inspire

For questions 1–9, darken the circle for the word or group of words that has the same or almost the same meaning as the underlined word.

1 A <u>boulevard</u> is a kind of—

A building

B watch

C street

D museum

2 An <u>abyss</u> is a—

F crater

G movie

H kind of dress

J fruit

3 <u>Vacant</u> means—

A colorful

B fresh

C occupied

D empty

4 A <u>jaunt</u> is—

F an experience

G an outing

H a problem

J an opportunity

5 To <u>convey</u> is to—

A build

B transport

C examine

D memorize

6 A <u>boutique</u> is a kind of—

F store

G designer

H show

J florist

7 To <u>recollect</u> is to—

A remember

B watch

C forget

D bargain

8 Someone who is <u>optimistic</u> is—

F discouraged

G hopeful

H sad

J funny

9 To <u>collapse</u> means to—

A fall down

B go around

C sell out

D blow up

TEST TIP

Look for prefixes, suffixes, and roots to find the meaning of unfamiliar words.

Answers

SA Ⓐ Ⓑ Ⓒ Ⓓ   2 Ⓕ Ⓖ Ⓗ Ⓙ   4 Ⓕ Ⓖ Ⓗ Ⓙ   6 Ⓕ Ⓖ Ⓗ Ⓙ   8 Ⓕ Ⓖ Ⓗ Ⓙ
1 Ⓐ Ⓑ Ⓒ Ⓓ   3 Ⓐ Ⓑ Ⓒ Ⓓ   5 Ⓐ Ⓑ Ⓒ Ⓓ   7 Ⓐ Ⓑ Ⓒ Ⓓ   9 Ⓐ Ⓑ Ⓒ Ⓓ

Sample B

> There are costumes in the old <u>trunk</u>.

In which sentence does <u>trunk</u> have the same meaning as it does in the sentence above?

A   The baby elephant raised its <u>trunk</u>.

B   Two squirrels ran down the tree <u>trunk</u>.

C   Put these boxes in the <u>trunk</u> of my car.

D   Grandmother's <u>trunk</u> is in the basement.

For questions 10–13, darken the circle for the sentence in which the underlined word means the same as it does in the sentence in the box.

10

> Will the town <u>recover</u> from the storm damage?

In which sentence does <u>recover</u> have the same meaning as it does in the sentence above?

F   Jill got some fabric to <u>recover</u> the cushion.

G   I will <u>recover</u> from the accident soon.

H   Will the police <u>recover</u> the stolen property?

J   Those recyling companies <u>recover</u> steel from old appliances.

11

> Does Matt exercise to stay <u>fit</u>?

In which sentence does <u>fit</u> have the same meaning as it does in the sentence above?

A   My clothes don't <u>fit</u> since I've grown.

B   Will that table <u>fit</u> here?

C   You need to be <u>fit</u> to enter that race.

D   Shoes that don't <u>fit</u> properly can hurt.

12

> A flood can <u>sweep</u> away everything in its path.

In which sentence does <u>sweep</u> have the same meaning as it does in the sentence above?

F   Our track team will <u>sweep</u> all the events.

G   Can you <u>sweep</u> aside your doubts?

H   Karl will <u>sweep</u> the gym floors.

J   The famous actress likes to <u>sweep</u> into a room.

13

> Her clothes were in a <u>mess</u> on the floor.

In which sentence does <u>mess</u> have the same meaning as it does in the sentence above?

A   I'll clean up this <u>mess</u> before I leave.

B   Please don't <u>mess</u> with my things!

C   She'll <u>mess</u> this up if she is in a hurry.

D   The soldiers met in the <u>mess</u> tent.

14

> Dad will <u>hang</u> the painting for me.

Write a new sentence in which <u>hang</u> has the same meaning as it does in the sentence above.

_____

_____

_____

_____

_____

_____

_____

GO ON ➡

Answers
SB Ⓐ Ⓑ Ⓒ Ⓓ   **10** Ⓕ Ⓖ Ⓗ Ⓙ   **11** Ⓐ Ⓑ Ⓒ Ⓓ   **12** Ⓕ Ⓖ Ⓗ Ⓙ   **13** Ⓐ Ⓑ Ⓒ Ⓓ

Sample C

We camped in the <u>grotto</u> under the cliffs. A <u>grotto</u> is—

A   a group of trees

B   a small cave

C   a simple hut

D   a forest preserve

For questions 15–20, darken the circle for the word or words that give the meaning of the underlined word.

15   It has been an extremely <u>brutal</u> winter with very cold temperatures. <u>Brutal</u> means—

A   harsh

B   windy

C   gentle

D   pleasant

16   Brass is an <u>alloy</u> of copper and zinc. An <u>alloy</u> is—

F   a type of plastic

G   a mixture of metals

H   a kind of sword

J   a kind of ore

17   The two interstate highways run in different directions, but they <u>intersect</u> in Atlanta. <u>Intersect</u> means—

A   end

B   run parallel

C   cross each other

D   begin

18   She offered a <u>feeble</u> excuse for her tardiness, but she could tell we didn't believe it. <u>Feeble</u> means—

F   truthful

G   excellent

H   exaggerated

J   weak

19   That sofa was <u>manufactured</u> in our new furniture factory. <u>Manufactured</u> means—

A   sold

B   designed

C   made

D   used

20   Brad took Jana's arm and <u>escorted</u> her down the runway. <u>Escorted</u> means—

F   accompanied

G   led

H   followed

J   carried

Write the following meanings:

21   Because Gerardo is organized and efficient, he is a <u>capable</u> office manager. <u>Capable</u> means—

_____

_____

_____

22   Marta smiled when she heard the joyful <u>clamor</u> coming from the playroom. <u>Clamor</u> means—

_____

_____

_____

_____

Answers

SC Ⓐ Ⓑ Ⓒ Ⓓ   **16** Ⓕ Ⓖ Ⓗ Ⓙ   **18** Ⓕ Ⓖ Ⓗ Ⓙ   **20** Ⓕ Ⓖ Ⓗ Ⓙ

15 Ⓐ Ⓑ Ⓒ Ⓓ   **17** Ⓐ Ⓑ Ⓒ Ⓓ   **19** Ⓐ Ⓑ Ⓒ Ⓓ

MATH PROBLEM-SOLVING PLAN

THE PROBLEM-SOLVING PLAN

When solving math problems follow these steps:

STEP 1: WHAT IS THE QUESTION/GOAL?

Read the problem. Decide what must be found. This is sometimes in the form of a question.

STEP 2: FIND THE FACTS

Locate the factual information in three different ways:

- A. **KEY FACTS** are the facts you need to solve the problem.
- B. **FACTS YOU DON'T NEED** are those facts that are not necessary for solving the problem.
- C. **ARE MORE FACTS NEEDED?** Decide if you have enough information to solve the problem.

STEP 3: SELECT A STRATEGY

Decide what strategies you might use, how you will use them, and then estimate what your answer will be. If one strategy doesn't help you to solve the problem, try another.

STEP 4: SOLVE

Apply the strategy according to your plan. Use an operation if necessary, and clearly indicate your answer.

STEP 5: DOES YOUR RESPONSE MAKE SENSE?

Write your answer in a complete sentence. Read the problem again. Check to see that your answer makes sense. Use estimation to check calculations.

TEST TIP

You can use this problem-solving plan to solve many different types of math problems. These steps help you get started on problems that seem confusing at first.

Directions: Use the problem-solving plan to solve this math problem.

PROBLEM/QUESTION:

Justine drives to her company's main office every day, Monday through Thursday. The trip is 20 miles one way. On Friday, she drives to the regional office. This trip is 50 miles one way. How many miles does Justine drive in three weeks?

STEP 1: WHAT IS THE QUESTION/GOAL?

_____

_____

_____

STEP 2: FIND THE FACTS

_____

_____

_____

STEP 3: SELECT A STRATEGY

_____

_____

_____

STEP 4: SOLVE

_____

_____

_____

STEP 5: DOES YOUR RESPONSE MAKE SENSE?

_____

_____

_____

Directions: Use the problem-solving plan to solve this math problem.

PROBLEM/QUESTION:

Ian began the week with $48. On Monday, he spent half of it. On Tuesday, he spent one-third of the amount he still had. On Wednesday, he spent one fourth of the money he still had. On Thursday, he spent one-sixth of the amount he still had. On what day did he spend the most money?

STEP 1: WHAT IS THE QUESTION/GOAL?

_____

_____

_____

STEP 2: FIND THE FACTS

_____

_____

_____

STEP 3: SELECT A STRATEGY

_____

_____

_____

STEP 4: SOLVE

_____

_____

_____

STEP 5: DOES YOUR RESPONSE MAKE SENSE?

_____

_____

_____

MATH PROBLEM SOLVING

UNDERSTANDING NUMBER RELATIONSHIPS

Directions: Darken the circle for the correct answer, or write in the answer.

> **TRY THIS**
>
> Read each problem carefully. Make sure you understand the question that is being asked. Then choose the best method to solve the problem.

Sample A

Which fraction is smallest in value?

A $\frac{1}{8}$

B $\frac{1}{5}$

C $\frac{3}{5}$

D $\frac{3}{8}$

> **THINK IT THROUGH**
>
> The correct answer is <u>A</u>. The fraction $\frac{1}{8}$ is smaller than the other fractions listed. Using the common denominator 40, $\frac{1}{8}$ becomes $\frac{5}{40}$, and the other fractions become $\frac{8}{40}, \frac{24}{40}$, and $\frac{15}{40}$.

STOP

---

1 What is the value of point X on the number line?

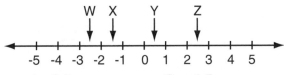

A 0.5

B 2.5

C −1.5

D −2.5

2 Each ▱ represents 0.01.

Which decimal is shown by the figure above?

F 1.25

G 12.5

H 0.0125

J 120.5

3 After picking berries, 4 friends compared the amounts of berries in their buckets. Juan's bucket was $\frac{2}{3}$ full, Jamie's bucket was $\frac{4}{5}$ full, Lenny's bucket was $\frac{3}{4}$ full, and Hazel's bucket was $\frac{3}{8}$ full. How would these amounts be arranged in order from greatest to least?

A $\frac{4}{5}, \frac{3}{4}, \frac{2}{3}, \frac{3}{8}$

B $\frac{2}{3}, \frac{3}{4}, \frac{3}{8}, \frac{4}{5}$

C $\frac{3}{8}, \frac{3}{4}, \frac{4}{5}, \frac{2}{3}$

D $\frac{3}{8}, \frac{2}{3}, \frac{4}{5}, \frac{3}{4}$

4 The thermometer shows the reading early this morning. By noon, the temperature had increased 15° from the early morning reading. What is the new reading?

STOP

Answers

SA Ⓐ Ⓑ Ⓒ Ⓓ   1 Ⓐ Ⓑ Ⓒ Ⓓ   2 Ⓕ Ⓖ Ⓗ Ⓙ   3 Ⓐ Ⓑ Ⓒ Ⓓ

Directions: Darken the circle for the correct answer, or write in the answer.

> **TRY THIS**
>
> Read the question twice before choosing your answer. Make sure you understand the question that is being asked. Think about which numbers stand for ones, tens, hundreds, and so on.

Sample A

The call number on this library catalog card is 612.48. What is the value of the 8 in this number?

A   8 ten-thousandths

B   8 thousandths

C   8 hundredths

D   8 tenths

612.48	Remembering Vietnam/Quy Luong
L	Luong, Quy
	Illustrations by Thuy Dang
	San Francisco: Freedom Rings Press,
	1990
	147 p. : ill. ; 23 cm.
	1. Vietnam. I. Luong, Quy. II. Title

> **THINK IT THROUGH**
>
> The correct answer is <u>C</u>. In the number 612.48, the 8 is in the hundredths place, so its value is <u>8 hundredths</u>. The 4 is in the tenths place.

---

1 Which of these means the same as 5^3?

A   15

B   125

C   8

D   243

2 One estimate for the distance from Earth to the Andromeda Galaxy is 2,300,000 light years. What is this distance expressed in scientific notation?

F 2.3×10^5

G 23×10^5

H 2.3×10^6

J $2^3 \times 10^7$

3 How would the product $3 \times 3 \times 7 \times 5 \times 5$ be expressed in exponential notation?

A $3^3 \times 7 \times 5^5$

B 2^3

C $3^2 \times 7 \times 5^2$

D 10^5

4 Look at the factor tree shown here. Notice the number of branches in the factor tree.

How many branches will the number 17 have in its completed factor tree?

_____

_____

_____

Answers

SA Ⓐ Ⓑ Ⓒ Ⓓ   1 Ⓐ Ⓑ Ⓒ Ⓓ   2 Ⓕ Ⓖ Ⓗ Ⓙ   3 Ⓐ Ⓑ Ⓒ Ⓓ

Directions: Darken the circle for the correct answer, or write in your answer.

> **TRY THIS**
>
> Check your work by making sure both sides of an equation are equal values. Try using all the answer choices in the problem to help you choose the correct solution.

Sample A

Which value of x makes the equation $x - 12 = 40$ correct?

A 60   C 45

B 52   D 38

THINK IT THROUGH The correct answer is <u>B</u>, <u>52</u>. Because the unknown number minus 12 equals 40, it is necessary to add 40 and 12 to find the unknown.

 STOP

---

1 Meg baked a chocolate cake. She knows that the cake contains 2,700 calories. She has cut the cake into 12 equal-sized pieces. If c represents the number of calories in one piece, which equation can she use to find the number of calories in each piece?

A $12 + c = 2,700$

B $12 \div c = 2,700$

C $12c = 2,700$

D $2700 - c = 12$

2 What is another way to write $6(a + 7)$?

F $(6 + a) \times (6 + 7)$

G $6a + 7$

H $7 \times (6 + a)$

J $(6 \times a) + (6 \times 7)$

3 It took Gene three times as long to paint one side of the fence as it took David to paint the other side. If h is the number of hours David painted, which expression shows the time spent by Gene painting?

A $3 \times h$

B $3 - h$

C $3 + h$

D $3 \div h$

4 Which of the following problems could be solved by the equation $2x = 36 + 52$?

F Greg has 36 trading cards. Harry has twice as many. How many cards does Harry have?

G Class A has 36 students, and Class B has twice as many students. How many more students are in Class B?

H The first plant is 36 inches tall, and the second plant is 52 inches tall. If their heights were doubled, how tall would they each be?

J Tank A has 36 fish, and Tank B has 52 fish. If the fish are divided equally between both tanks, how many fish will be in each tank?

5 Clara's pay from her paper route is based on the expression \$15 + \$0.10p, where p is the number of papers she delivers during the week. What would her weekly pay be if she delivers 315 papers each week?

_____

_____

_____

_____

_____

STOP

Answers

SA Ⓐ Ⓑ Ⓒ Ⓓ   1 Ⓐ Ⓑ Ⓒ Ⓓ   2 Ⓕ Ⓖ Ⓗ Ⓙ   3 Ⓐ Ⓑ Ⓒ Ⓓ   4 Ⓕ Ⓖ Ⓗ Ⓙ

Directions: Darken the circle for the correct answer, or write in the answer.

> **TRY THIS**
>
> Read each question carefully. Determine the nature of the pattern or relationship in the problem. Try using all the answer choices in the problem. Then choose the answer that you think best answers the question.

Sample A

Look at the pattern shown here. Which number is missing?

101, 105, 109, ☐, 117

A 113   C 110

B 112   D 107

> **THINK IT THROUGH**
>
> The correct answer is <u>A</u>. The pattern shows that each number increases by 4. Therefore, to find the missing number, add 109 and 4 to get the answer, <u>113</u>.

1 A special machine changes numbers according to a certain rule. The *out* number in the table shows the result when the rule is applied to the *in* number.

In	5	45	20
Out	1	9	4

What number will 30 be changed to?

A 150

B 35

C 25

D 6

2 In a basketball free-throw contest held at the high school, Rudy made 4 out of 5 free throws. At this rate, how many free throws could he expect to make in 25 tries?

_____

_____

_____

_____

_____

_____

3 Fran bought 6 yards of blue tapestry material. She used it to upholster 3 chairs. How much of the material would she need to upholster 7 chairs?

F 21 yards

G 16 yards

H 14 yards

J 10 yards

4 Shown here are the first three figures in a pattern. How many stars would be in the seventh figure of the pattern?

★ ★   ★ ★ ★   ★ ★ ★ ★
  ★   ★ ★   ★ ★ ★
★ ★   ★ ★ ★   ★ ★ ★ ★

A 20

B 23

C 26

D 28

> **TEST TIP**
>
> Use scratch paper to extend patterns and check your answers.

Answers
SA Ⓐ Ⓑ Ⓒ Ⓓ   1 Ⓐ Ⓑ Ⓒ Ⓓ   3 Ⓕ Ⓖ Ⓗ Ⓙ   4 Ⓐ Ⓑ Ⓒ Ⓓ

Directions: Darken the circle for the correct answer, or write in the answer.

> **TRY THIS**
>
> Read each question twice before choosing your answer. Study any given tables or graphs to help you choose the correct answer.

Sample A

Two pennies are tossed into the air. What is the probability they will match either heads-heads or tails-tails when they land?

A $\frac{1}{1}$ C $\frac{1}{4}$

B $\frac{1}{2}$ D $\frac{1}{8}$

> **THINK IT THROUGH**
>
> The correct answer is <u>B</u>. There are four possible outcomes: heads-heads, tails-tails, heads-tails, and tails-heads. Two of these four possibilities will match. That makes the correct answer a probability of $\frac{2}{4}$, or $\frac{1}{2}$.

STOP

---

1 Two six-sided number cubes, each numbered 1 through 6, are rolled together. What is the probability that they will land with the numbers on the top face having a sum greater than 10?

A 1 out of 6

B 1 out of 12

C 2 out of 36

D 10 out of 30

2 These are Yung's bowling scores for the past month.

192	148	192
150	175	202
269	225	240
148	121	192

What is Yung's bowling average?

_____

_____

3 According to this graph, which two energy sources together account for nearly one half?

SOURCES OF ENERGY

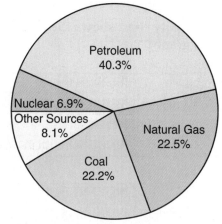

F Nuclear and natural gas

G Coal and other sources

H Petroleum and coal

J Natural gas and coal

4 Helen has a choice of 3 colors of paint, 4 kinds of curtains, and 2 colors of carpet to decorate her apartment. How many different combinations of paint, curtains, and carpets can she use?

A 9   C 24

B 18   D 36

STOP

Answers
SA Ⓐ Ⓑ Ⓒ Ⓓ   **1** Ⓐ Ⓑ Ⓒ Ⓓ   **3** Ⓕ Ⓖ Ⓗ Ⓙ   **4** Ⓐ Ⓑ Ⓒ Ⓓ

Miguel earned $20 at his part-time job. The following graph shows how he spent the money. Study the graph. Then answer questions 5 and 6.

Miguel's Earnings

30% Lunch Out
45% Savings
20% Magazines
5% Owed to Mom

5 What percent of his money did Miguel spend on lunch and magazines combined?

F 50% H 20%

G 30% J 25%

6 Which tally chart shows the data in the circle graph?

A

Lunch	̶N̶N̶ ̶N̶N̶ ̶N̶N̶ ̶N̶N̶
Magazines	̶N̶N̶ ̶N̶N̶ ̶N̶N̶ ̶N̶N̶ ̶N̶N̶ ̶N̶N̶
Owed	̶N̶N̶
Savings	̶N̶N̶ ̶N̶N̶ ̶N̶N̶ ̶N̶N̶ ̶N̶N̶ ̶N̶N̶ ̶N̶N̶ ̶N̶N̶ ̶N̶N̶

B

Lunch	̶N̶N̶ ̶N̶N̶ ̶N̶N̶ ̶N̶N̶ ̶N̶N̶ ̶N̶N̶
Magazines	̶N̶N̶ ̶N̶N̶ ̶N̶N̶ ̶N̶N̶
Owed	̶N̶N̶
Savings	̶N̶N̶ ̶N̶N̶ ̶N̶N̶ ̶N̶N̶ ̶N̶N̶ ̶N̶N̶ ̶N̶N̶ ̶N̶N̶ ̶N̶N̶

C

Lunch	̶N̶N̶ ̶N̶N̶ ̶N̶N̶
Magazines	̶N̶N̶ ̶N̶N̶
Owed	̶N̶N̶
Savings	̶N̶N̶ ̶N̶N̶ ̶N̶N̶ ̶N̶N̶ ̶N̶N̶

D

Lunch	̶N̶N̶ ̶N̶N̶ ̶N̶N̶ ̶N̶N̶
Magazines	̶N̶N̶ ̶N̶N̶ ̶N̶N̶ ̶N̶N̶ ̶N̶N̶
Owed	̶N̶N̶
Savings	̶N̶N̶ ̶N̶N̶ ̶N̶N̶ ̶N̶N̶ ̶N̶N̶

The graph below shows the prices of two stocks over a period of time. Use the graph to answer questions 7–9.

Stock Values During a 12-month Period

—●— Abbott Aluminum Works   —■— Claney Steel Inc.

7 What was the greatest price difference between Abbott and Claney stock during the period shown on the graph?

F $30 H $19

G $27 J $15

8 Ella bought 20 shares of Claney stock in April and sold them in October at the current price at that time. About how much profit did she make?

A About $100

B About $220

C About $285

D About $325

9 If Larry bought 12 shares of Abbott stock on May 4, what did he pay for the stock?

_____

_____

_____

_____

STOP

Answers

5 F G H J   6 A B C D   7 F G H J   8 A B C D

68

Directions: Darken the circle for the correct answer, or write in the answer.

TRY THIS Read each question carefully. Look for key words such as <u>area</u>, <u>volume</u>, <u>radius</u>, and <u>diameter</u>. Use the objects shown or named to help you answer each question.

Sample A

Uncle Tony's vegetable garden is in the shape of a square. What is the area of his garden?

A   14 sq ft

B   28 sq ft

C   56 sq ft

D   196 sq ft

14 ft

THINK IT THROUGH The correct answer is <u>D</u>, <u>196 sq ft</u>. To determine the area of a square, multiply side by side: $A = s2$. So, $14 \times 14 = 196$.

---

1   Michiko's mother stores buttons in the box shown here. What is the volume of the box? (Use $V = l \times w \times h$.)

4 in.

5 in.

8 in.

A   160 cu in.

B   80 cu in.

C   73 cu in.

D   17 cu in.

2   An ice-skating rink is shown here. What is the area of the rink? (Use $A = lw$.)

30 ft

20 ft

_____

_____

3   Rectangle FGDE is similar to rectangle ECBA. Which line segments are perpendicular?

F $\overline{FG}$ and $\overline{DC}$

G $\overline{AB}$ and $\overline{ED}$

H $\overline{EA}$ and $\overline{AB}$

J $\overline{CB}$ and $\overline{FE}$

4   An apple pie has a diameter of 9 inches. What is its circumference rounded to the nearest whole number? (Use $C = \pi d$ and $\pi = 3.14$.)

A   14 inches

B   28 inches

C   36 inches

D   57 inches

Answers
SA Ⓐ Ⓑ Ⓒ Ⓓ   1 Ⓐ Ⓑ Ⓒ Ⓓ   3 Ⓕ Ⓖ Ⓗ Ⓙ   4 Ⓐ Ⓑ Ⓒ Ⓓ

5 Which of these angles appears to be an obtuse angle?

F

G

H

J

6 Which transformation moves the figure from position A to position B?

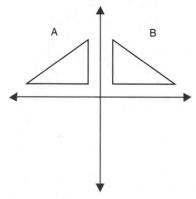

A Rotation

B Translation

C Reflection

D Extension

7 The diameter of this circle is represented by which line segment?

F $\overline{XA}$

G $\overline{XC}$

H $\overline{BX}$

J $\overline{AC}$

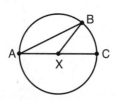

8 Which of these pattern pieces would not form a cube if folded along the dotted lines?

A

B

C

D

9 The distance from the edge to the center of a circle is called the

_____

_____

_____

STOP

Answers
5 Ⓕ Ⓖ Ⓗ Ⓙ   **6** Ⓐ Ⓑ Ⓒ Ⓓ   **7** Ⓕ Ⓖ Ⓗ Ⓙ   **8** Ⓐ Ⓑ Ⓒ Ⓓ

Directions: Darken the circle for the correct answer, or write in the answer.

TRY THIS

Read the question carefully. Study the answer choices. Sometimes more than one answer looks correct. Use the objects shown or named to help you answer each question.

Sample A

Which of these units is used to measure length on a ruler?

A degrees

B kilograms

C centimeters

D liters

THINK IT THROUGH

The correct answer is C. Degrees are used to measure temperature, kilograms are used to measure mass, liters are used to measure capacity, and centimeters are used to measure length.

STOP

---

1   Mr. Baker cooked $4\frac{1}{2}$ quarts of rice. How many 1-cup servings did this make?

A $5\frac{1}{2}$ cups

B 9 cups

C 10 cups

D 18 cups

2   The scale model shown here represents a rectangular parking lot.

Scale: 1 cm represents 15 m

Use your centimeter ruler to help answer this question. What is the actual length of each of the 2 long sides of the parking lot?

F 4 meters

G 15 meters

H 60 meters

J 90 meters

3   Use your inch ruler to help answer this question. What is the approximate length of one side of this toy block?

Scale: $\frac{1}{2}$ inch represents 2 inches

_____

_____

_____

_____

_____

4   Tammy caught a catfish that was $2\frac{2}{3}$ feet long. How many inches long was it?

A 16 inches

B 26 inches

C 29 inches

D 32 inches

GO ON ➡

Answers
SA Ⓐ Ⓑ Ⓒ Ⓓ   1 Ⓐ Ⓑ Ⓒ Ⓓ   2 Ⓕ Ⓖ Ⓗ Ⓙ   4 Ⓐ Ⓑ Ⓒ Ⓓ

5 How high off the ground is the kite?

F 300 feet

G 245 feet

H 150 feet

J 145 feet

6 The testing session began at 8:45 A.M. The time limit on the first test was 35 minutes and the time limit on the second test was 40 minutes. There was a 10-minute break between the tests. At what time did the session end?

A 10:00 A.M.

B 10:10 A.M.

C 10:25 A.M.

D 11:05 A.M.

7 Gino and Claire went to see a movie last night. The movie began at 7:30 P.M. It lasted $1\frac{3}{4}$ hours. What time did the movie end?

F 9:15 P.M.

G 9:20 P.M.

H 9:30 P.M.

J 9:45 P.M.

TEST TIP

It is crucial to follow every step in a multistep problem. To answer question 6, first find the total time for the session, including the break. Then you can find the elapsed time.

8 On a map of a cross-country ski area, 1 inch represents 3 miles. What is the distance between two turn-around areas 4 inches apart on the map?

A 3 miles

B 4 miles

C 7 miles

D 12 miles

9 The picture shows that Miyoshi is standing 6 yards from the tree. How many feet is that?

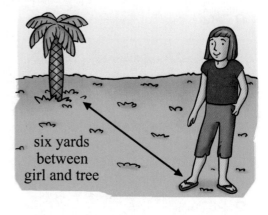

six yards between girl and tree

_____

_____

_____

_____

_____

_____

10 Marty's soccer team starts its practice at 4:30 P.M. It ends at 5:15 P.M. How long does Marty's soccer team practice?

_____

_____

_____

_____

_____

_____

STOP

Answers

5 Ⓕ Ⓖ Ⓗ Ⓙ   **6** Ⓐ Ⓑ Ⓒ Ⓓ   **7** Ⓕ Ⓖ Ⓗ Ⓙ   **8** Ⓐ Ⓑ Ⓒ Ⓓ

Directions: Darken the circle for the correct answer, or write in the answer.

TRY THIS Study each problem carefully. Think about what each problem is asking, then decide on the best strategy to find the answer.

Sample A

A local factory produces tuners for car radios. Of the 400 tuners produced each hour, 30 are damaged. How many undamaged tuners does the factory produce in an 8-hour day?

A 370

B 430

C 2,960

D 3,440

THINK IT THROUGH The correct answer is C, 2,960. If 30 out of 400 produced each hour are damaged, then 370 are undamaged. To find how many undamaged tuners are produced in 8 hours, multiply 370 times 8 to get 2,960.

STOP

1 Joyce decorated a tree in her yard with popcorn for birds to eat. On the first branch, she hung a string with 4 pieces of popcorn. On the second branch, she hung a string with 8 pieces of popcorn, and on the third branch a string with 16 pieces of popcorn. If she continued this pattern, how many pieces of popcorn would be on the string that she hung on the fifth branch?

A 18

B 24

C 32

D 64

2 During the first three hours at the car wash, 15 fewer cars were washed during the first hour than during the third hour. During the second hour, 5 more cars were washed than during the first hour. During the third hour, 40 cars were washed. How many cars were washed during the second hour?

_____

_____

_____

_____

3 Frances wants to provide each of her students with 5 strips of leather for an art project. She buys the leather strips at a craft store for $0.89 each. What other information is needed to learn how much Frances pays for the leather strips?

F the length of each strip

G the number of students in her class

H the number of strips in a package

J the colors of strips available

Use the figure shown here to answer question 4.

				12	Row 1
			14	16	Row 2
		18	20	22	Row 3
	24	26	28	30	Row 4
32	34	36	38	40	Row 5
					Row 6

4 Fill in the numbers to complete Row 6.

STOP

Answers
SA Ⓐ Ⓑ Ⓒ Ⓓ   1 Ⓐ Ⓑ Ⓒ Ⓓ   3 Ⓕ Ⓖ Ⓗ Ⓙ

Directions: Darken the circle for the correct answer, or write in the answer.

> **TRY THIS**
>
> Round numbers when you estimate. For some problems, there are no exact answers. Then you should take your best guess. You can check your answer by using the numbers given in the problem.

Sample A

Lucas bought 3 magazines: one for $3.25, one for $2.75, and one for $4.57. With tax included, about how much did Lucas spend?

A $9

B $11

C $13

D $15

> **THINK IT THROUGH**
>
> The correct answer is B, $11.00. Round $3.25 to $3.00, $2.75 to $3.00, and $4.57 to $5.00. The sum of these estimates is $11.00, which would include about $0.80 in tax. Check by adding $3.25, $2.75, $4.57 and $0.80. The sum is $11.37.

🛑 STOP

---

1 Terri is working on a class project. She cut a pine board into 12 equal parts. She used 9 of the pieces to build some shelves. About what percent of the board is left?

A 6%

B 9%

C 12%

D 25%

2 Mr. Petrovich has 11,200 coins in his collection. He plans to add another 1,500 to his collection this year. What is the best estimate of the number of coins Mr. Petrovich will have at the end of this year?

F 11,000 coins

G 12,000 coins

H 13,000 coins

J 14,000 coins

3 Ellen enjoys exercise. It usually takes her 9 minutes to jog a mile. What is a reasonable estimate of the time it would take Ellen to jog 5 miles?

A less than 30 minutes

B between 30 and 40 minutes

C between 40 and 50 minutes

D more than 50 minutes

4 On Liz's vacation she planned to travel $297\frac{3}{4}$ kilometers on a train. If the train had traveled $74\frac{1}{2}$ kilometers, what is the best estimate of the number of kilometers she had left to travel?

F $120\frac{1}{4}$ kilometers

G 225 kilometers

H 270 kilometers

J 370 kilometers

5 This chart shows some of the rivers in Africa.

River	Length
Nile River	4,145 miles
Limpopo River	1,100 miles
Niger River	2,600 miles
Orange River	1,300 miles
Zambezi River	1,650 miles

About how much shorter is the Orange River than the Nile River?

_____

_____

_____

 STOP

Answers

SA Ⓐ Ⓑ Ⓒ Ⓓ   **1** Ⓐ Ⓑ Ⓒ Ⓓ   **2** Ⓕ Ⓖ Ⓗ Ⓙ   **3** Ⓐ Ⓑ Ⓒ Ⓓ   **4** Ⓕ Ⓖ Ⓗ Ⓙ

Sample A

Which fraction is greatest in value?

$$\frac{2}{12} \qquad \frac{2}{4} \qquad \frac{2}{2} \qquad \frac{2}{6}$$

A $\frac{2}{12}$ C $\frac{2}{2}$

B $\frac{2}{4}$ D $\frac{2}{6}$

For questions 1–38, darken the circle for the correct answer, or write in the answer.

1 The stock number on an item is 54.763. What is the value of the 3 in 54.763?

    A 3 ten-thousandths

    B 3 thousandths

    C 3 hundredths

    D 3 tenths

2 Light travels at a speed of 186,282 miles per second. How could this number be expressed in scientific notation?

    F $1,862.82 \times 10^3$ H 1.86282×10^4

    G 1.86282×10^5 J 186.282×10^{-3}

3 What is the value of point B on the number line?

    A $2\frac{1}{3}$ C $3\frac{2}{3}$

    B $\frac{1}{3}$ D 4

4 Which fraction does not have the same value as the other fractions?

$$6\frac{2}{3} \qquad \frac{20}{3} \qquad 6\frac{9}{12} \qquad 6\frac{4}{6}$$

    F $6\frac{2}{3}$ H $6\frac{9}{12}$

    G $\frac{20}{3}$ J $6\frac{4}{6}$

5 Which problem could be solved by the equation $x = 0.3 \times 200$?

    A Three hamburgers cost $2. How much does one cost?

    B A theater holds 200 people. How many people would be able to attend 3 showings of a movie?

    C The regular fare of $200 for a plane ticket was just reduced by 30%. What would the savings be?

    D The temperature in an oven was 200 degrees. It was then increased by 0.3 degrees. What is the current oven temperature?

6 Which decimal shows the part of this figure that is shaded?

    F 5.8   H 0.058

    G 0.58   J 5.08

7 In what way are the numbers in the oval related?

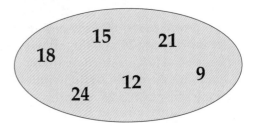

_____

_____

_____

_____

GO ON ⇒

Answers
SA Ⓐ Ⓑ Ⓒ Ⓓ   2 Ⓕ Ⓖ Ⓗ Ⓙ   4 Ⓕ Ⓖ Ⓗ Ⓙ   6 Ⓕ Ⓖ Ⓗ Ⓙ
  1 Ⓐ Ⓑ Ⓒ Ⓓ   3 Ⓐ Ⓑ Ⓒ Ⓓ   5 Ⓐ Ⓑ Ⓒ Ⓓ

75

8 If $32 = 5d + 7$, what is the value of d?

A 2

B 4

C 5

D 8

9 Andy has the 2 cubes shown here. They have the numbers 1, 2, 3, 4, 5, and 6 on their faces. If he rolls the cubes together, what is the probability that the 2 numbers showing at the top of the cubes will total 6 when added together?

F $\frac{1}{4}$

G $\frac{5}{24}$

H $\frac{1}{6}$

J $\frac{5}{36}$

10 Ray uses 4 boards to build 1 step, 10 boards to build 2 steps, and 18 boards to build 3 steps. Following this pattern, how many boards would you expect Ray to use to build 5 steps?

_____

_____

_____

_____

_____

11 At a recent marshmallow-eating contest, the winner ate 20 marshmallows in 5 minutes. At that rate, how many marshmallows would the winner eat if the contest has lasted 25 minutes?

A 120

B 100

C 40

D 25

12 Emma bought 2 pairs of socks for $2.95 each. She bought a pair of shoes that cost 8 times as much as a pair of socks. Which expression could be used to determine the cost of the shoes?

F $(8 - 2) + \$2.95$

G $(\$2.95 \times 2) + (\$2.95 \times 8)$

H $(8 + 2) - \$2.95$

J $\$2.95 \times 8$

13 The average (mean) temperature for 4 days was 74 degrees. Which set of temperatures could reasonably show the exact temperatures for the 4 days?

A 74°, 75°, 76°, 77°

B 74°, 72°, 72°, 70°

C 78°, 75°, 74°, 74°

D 72°, 76°, 68°, 80°

14 The camera club is responsible for decorating one of the bulletin boards at school. They change the bulletin board every month. They have three colors of border trim, 5 background colors, and 2 styles of lettering to choose from. If they use 1 border, 1 background color, and 1 style of lettering at a time, how many months of bulletin-board combinations can they make?

F 30 months

G 15 months

H 10 months

J 6 months

GO ON

Answers

8 Ⓐ Ⓑ Ⓒ Ⓓ   11 Ⓐ Ⓑ Ⓒ Ⓓ   13 Ⓐ Ⓑ Ⓒ Ⓓ

9 Ⓕ Ⓖ Ⓗ Ⓙ   12 Ⓕ Ⓖ Ⓗ Ⓙ   14 Ⓕ Ⓖ Ⓗ Ⓙ

This table shows the prices of four different kinds of markers. Study the table. Then answer questions 15–17.

Markers		
Kind	Number in box	Price per box
Wide tip	6	$3.00
Narrow tip	10	$3.50
Pastel colors	7	$5.50
Neon colors	5	$5.75
Washable	12	$5.40

15 Becky spent $9.25 for markers. Which two kinds of markers did she buy?

   A wide tip and washable

   B pastel colors and wide tip

   C neon colors and narrow tip

   D washable and pastel colors

16 How many more washable markers are in a box than pastel colors?

   F 5

   G 6

   H 7

   J 19

17 Juan bought a box of markers for which the cost of one marker was the lowest priced of the five kinds. Which kind of marker did he buy?

_____

_____

_____

_____

_____

Study the following graph. Then answer questions 18–20.

RECYCLING IN CENTER CITY

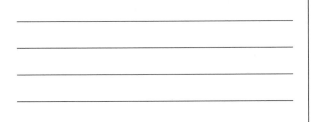

18 In what year did the people of Center City begin to recycle glass?

   A 1970   **C** 1985

   B 1980   **D** 1990

19 In what year did the people of Center City recycle four times as much newspaper as glass?

   F 1975   **H** 1985

   G 1980   **J** 1990

20 Which of the following conclusions can be made about Center City?

   A Recycling is declining in Center City.

   B Center City residents need to build a new park.

   C Recycling has become important to the residents of Center City.

   D Center City residents will probably stop recycling newspapers.

GO ON

Answers
15 Ⓐ Ⓑ Ⓒ Ⓓ   **16** Ⓕ Ⓖ Ⓗ Ⓙ   **18** Ⓐ Ⓑ Ⓒ Ⓓ   **19** Ⓕ Ⓖ Ⓗ Ⓙ   **20** Ⓐ Ⓑ Ⓒ Ⓓ

21 Which edge of the cube shown here is parallel to edge CD?

F $\overline{CG}$

G $\overline{AE}$

H $\overline{EF}$

J $\overline{BD}$

22 Wendy wanted to sew a new tablecloth for her round table. The radius of the table is 18 inches. What is the approximate circumference of the table? (Use C = πd and π = 3.14.)

A about 113 inches

B about 92 inches

C about 72 inches

D about 57 inches

23 There are 4 red beads, 8 yellow beads, and 2 pink beads in a bag. If one bead is picked at random from the bag, what is the probability that it will be red?

F $\frac{1}{2}$

G $\frac{2}{5}$

H $\frac{2}{7}$

J $\frac{1}{4}$

24 The diameter of this circle is represented by which line segment?

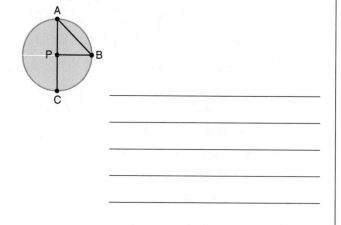

_____

_____

_____

_____

_____

_____

25 Which ordered pair in the park represents the location of the jungle gym?

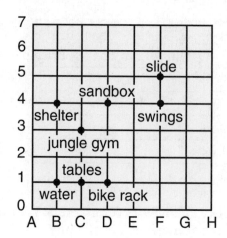

A (C, 2)

B (D, 3)

C (B, 4)

D (C, 3)

26 Which transformation moves the figure from position A to position B?

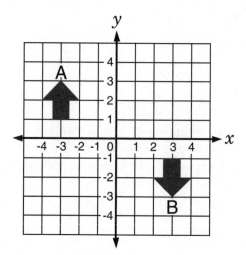

F reflection

G rotation

H translation

J extension

GO ON

27 Joan's piano lesson begins at 3:35. It ends at 4:05. How many minutes long is the lesson?

A 45 minutes

B 40 minutes

C 35 minutes

D 30 minutes

28 The scale model shown here represents the circular foundation of an 18th-century lighthouse in southern England.

Scale: 1 inch represents 16 feet

Use your inch ruler to help answer this question. What is the actual diameter of the foundation of the lighthouse?

F 14 feet

G 20 feet

H 28 feet

J 36 feet

29 A commuter train left the Shady Grove depot at 6:53 A.M. for a trip to Pecan Gap that takes 1 hour and 16 minutes. At what time should the train arrive at its destination?

_____

_____

_____

30 Juanita competes in races 4 times a year. It takes her between 30 and 35 minutes to run a $4\frac{1}{2}$-mile race. What would be a reasonable time for her to run a $2\frac{1}{4}$-mile race?

A between $6\frac{3}{4}$ and 9 minutes

B between 8 and 10 minutes

C between 15 and 20 minutes

D between 50 and 60 minutes

31 Swimming lessons at the local park district swimming pool cost $18.00 for 2 weeks of lessons. What is the best estimate of the total cost for 7 people to take swimming lessons at the pool?

F $30

G $70

H $90

J $140

32 Drew was leveling a table. One corner had to be raised $\frac{3}{4}$ inch. He had some pieces of wood $\frac{1}{16}$ inch thick. How many pieces of wood would he need to use for the corner to make the table level?

_____

_____

TEST TIP

Remember the rule for dividing fractions: Multiply the first fraction by the reciprocal of the second. To find the reciprocal, turn the fraction over by switching the numerator and denominator. For example, to answer question 32, you can divide $\frac{3}{4}$ by $\frac{1}{16}$. The reciprocal of $\frac{1}{16}$ is $\frac{16}{1}$. So $\frac{3}{4} \times \frac{16}{1} = \frac{48}{4} = 12$.

GO ON

33 The temperature outside rose 41 degrees during a 12-hour period. If the temperature rose the same number of degrees every hour, what is a good estimate of the number of degrees the temperature rose each hour?

A 2 degrees

B 3 degrees

C 6 degrees

D 7 degrees

34 About how far would a bird fly from Belton to Trell according to the map shown here?

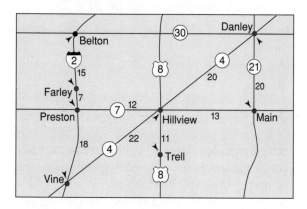

_____ miles

35 How many cubes are in this stack?

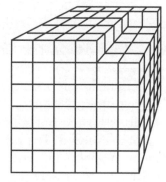

F 30

G 160

H 172

J 196

36 There are 24 parking spaces in each row in a parking lot. What information is needed to find the maximum number of parking spaces in the parking lot?

A the number of cars parked in each row

B the area of the parking lot

C the number of parking rows

D the number of empty parking spaces

37 Each square-shaped box in the pattern shown here decreases in length and width by $\frac{1}{2}$ unit each time. If Box 1 originally measured 12 by 12 units, what would be the dimensions of Box 9?

F 1 by 1 unit

G 8 by 8 units

H 5 by 5 units

J 10 by 10 units

38 Brand A laundry detergent costs more than Brand D. Brand D costs less than Brand X. Brand Z costs more than Brand A. Which of the following is most likely true?

A Brand Z costs more than Brand D.

B Brand X and Brand A cost the same.

C Brand Z costs less than Brand X.

D Brand A costs more than Brand X.

STOP

Answers

33 Ⓐ Ⓑ Ⓒ Ⓓ   **35** Ⓕ Ⓖ Ⓗ Ⓙ   **36** Ⓐ Ⓑ Ⓒ Ⓓ   **37** Ⓕ Ⓖ Ⓗ Ⓙ   **38** Ⓐ Ⓑ Ⓒ Ⓓ

Directions: Darken the circle for the correct answer. Darken the circle for NH (Not Here) if the correct answer is not given.

TRY THIS

Check the answer to a division problem by multiplying. Multiply your answer by the divisor in the problem. That answer should equal the larger number in the problem.

Sample A

$1.5\overline{)45}$

A 3
B 300
C 30
D 0.3
E NH

THINK IT THROUGH

The correct answer is <u>C</u>, <u>30</u>. First, move the decimal in 1.5 to 15. Next, move the decimal one place in 45 to 450, and write the decimal in the quotient. Then, divide as with whole numbers. Last, check the answer by multiplying 30 by 1.5.

STOP

1   $10\frac{1}{4} - 2\frac{3}{4} =$

A $8\frac{1}{2}$
B $8\frac{3}{4}$
C $7\frac{1}{4}$
D 13
E NH

2   $43\overline{)8285}$

F 190
G $192\frac{29}{43}$
H $191\frac{42}{43}$
J $192\frac{12}{43}$
K NH

3   852
  $\times\ 29$

A 24,708
B 24,372
C 24,608
D 14,708
E NH

4   $0.7\overline{)0.56}$

F 0.8
G 8
H 80
J 0.08
K NH

5   $3.84 \times 4.6 =$

A 3.840
B 17.664
C 176.64
D 27.664
E NH

6   $\frac{1}{5} \div \frac{1}{8} =$

F $\frac{1}{40}$
G $1\frac{3}{8}$
H $\frac{3}{5}$
J $1\frac{3}{5}$
K NH

STOP

Answers
SA (A)(B)(C)(D)(E)   2 (F)(G)(H)(J)(K)   4 (F)(G)(H)(J)(K)   6 (F)(G)(H)(J)(K)
1 (A)(B)(C)(D)(E)   3 (A)(B)(C)(D)(E)   5 (A)(B)(C)(D)(E)

USING COMPUTATION IN CONTEXT

Directions: Darken the circle for the correct answer. Darken the circle for NH (Not Here) if the correct answer is not given.

TRY THIS

Read the word problem carefully. Then set up the word problem as a computation problem. Solve the problem and compare it to the answer choices.

Sample A

Pat's rope measured 54 feet long, and Nick's rope was 65 feet long. What is the total length of the ropes?

- A 100 feet
- B 109 feet
- C 119 feet
- D 11 feet
- E NH

THINK IT THROUGH

The correct answer is C, 119 feet. To find the combined length of the two ropes, add 54 feet and 65 feet to get 119 feet.

 STOP

---

1 Mrs. Schultz's car has a gas tank that holds $12\frac{1}{2}$ gallons of gas. She used $\frac{1}{5}$ of a tank of gas. How many gallons did she use?

- A $2\frac{1}{2}$ gallons
- B $3\frac{1}{2}$ gallons
- C 4 gallons
- D $3\frac{3}{4}$ gallons
- E NH

2 Gwen was planting tomato plants in a row $6\frac{2}{3}$ yards long. She put the plants $\frac{2}{3}$ yard apart. How many plants were in the row?

- F $8\frac{2}{3}$
- G 9
- H 10
- J $7\frac{1}{3}$
- K NH

3 Alex spent $2.40 for cough medicine, $1.29 for cough drops, and $0.79 for tissues. What was the total cost of these items?

- A $3.88
- B $3.47
- C $4.48
- D $5.48
- E NH

4 At an arts and crafts fair, 65% of the vendors are selling either wooden handicrafts or paintings. What is that percent rounded to a compatible fraction?

- F $\frac{1}{3}$
- G $\frac{1}{2}$
- H $\frac{2}{3}$
- J $\frac{3}{4}$
- K NH

STOP

Answers

SA Ⓐ Ⓑ Ⓒ Ⓓ Ⓔ   2 Ⓕ Ⓖ Ⓗ Ⓙ Ⓚ   4 Ⓕ Ⓖ Ⓗ Ⓙ Ⓚ

1 Ⓐ Ⓑ Ⓒ Ⓓ Ⓔ   3 Ⓐ Ⓑ Ⓒ Ⓓ Ⓔ

Sample A

$\frac{2}{3} \div \frac{5}{6} =$

A $\frac{5}{9}$

B $\frac{3}{5}$

C $1\frac{1}{4}$

D $\frac{5}{6}$

E NH

STOP

Sample B

At the bowling alley Gina scored 133 in her first game, 146 in her second game, and 138 in her third game. What were Gina's total points for the 3 games?

F 371

G 408

H 417

J 517

K NH

STOP

For questions 1–14, darken the circle for the correct answer. If the correct answer is not given, darken the circle for NH (Not Here). If no choices are given, write in the answer.

1

$8.4 \times 0.934 =$

A 78.456

B 7.8456

C 0.78456

D 784.56

E NH

2

$44\overline{)8085}$

F $183\frac{3}{4}$

G $183\frac{23}{44}$

H $182\frac{34}{44}$

J 183

K NH

3

$6.183 \times 2.4 =$

A 14.8392

B 1.48392

C 0.148392

D 148.392

E NH

4

$2\frac{1}{3}$
$+ 4\frac{5}{12}$

F $6\frac{2}{5}$

G $6\frac{1}{2}$

H $6\frac{3}{4}$

J $6\frac{5}{6}$

K NH

5

$8\frac{2}{5} - 3\frac{7}{10} =$

A $4\frac{7}{10}$

B $12\frac{1}{10}$

C $3\frac{7}{10}$

D $3\frac{2}{5}$

E NH

6

$0.8\overline{)0.72}$

F 9

G 90

H 0.9

J 0.09

K NH

7

648
$\times 33$

A 3888

B 20,384

C 21,384

D 21,284

E NH

8

706
$\times 285$

_____

_____

_____

GO ON ➡

Answers

SA Ⓐ Ⓑ Ⓒ Ⓓ Ⓔ   2 Ⓕ Ⓖ Ⓗ Ⓙ Ⓚ   5 Ⓐ Ⓑ Ⓒ Ⓓ Ⓔ

SB Ⓕ Ⓖ Ⓗ Ⓙ Ⓚ   3 Ⓐ Ⓑ Ⓒ Ⓓ Ⓔ   6 Ⓕ Ⓖ Ⓗ Ⓙ Ⓚ

1 Ⓐ Ⓑ Ⓒ Ⓓ Ⓔ   4 Ⓕ Ⓖ Ⓗ Ⓙ Ⓚ   7 Ⓐ Ⓑ Ⓒ Ⓓ Ⓔ

9 Julius and his family drove to New Orleans. On the way there, they drove 298 miles. They took a shorter route back and drove 286 miles. How many miles did they drive altogether?

F 384

G 484

H 584

J 12

K NH

10 The tallest seventh-grade boy is $70\frac{3}{8}$ inches tall. What is his height rounded to the nearest half inch?

A 70 inches

B 71 inches

C $70\frac{1}{2}$ inches

D 80 inches

E NH

11 Last month, Juanita ran the 100-meter dash in 12.56 seconds. Yesterday, she ran the 100-meter dash in 11.97 seconds. By how much did her time improve from last month?

F 0.59 seconds

G 0.65 seconds

H 0.69 seconds

J 0.75 seconds

K NH

TEST TIP

Learn decimal equivalents for common fractions. This will help you check fraction questions with a calculator. For example, $\frac{1}{4}$ = 0.25, $\frac{1}{5}$ = 0.2, and $\frac{1}{8}$ = 0.125.

---

12 Lauren read 3 books last weekend. She made this table to show the time she spent reading.

Lauren's Weekend Reading			
Books	1	2	3
Hours	$4\frac{3}{4}$	$3\frac{1}{2}$	$1\frac{1}{4}$

How many hours did Lauren spend reading the 3 books?

A $8\frac{3}{4}$ hours

B $8\frac{1}{4}$ hours

C $7\frac{1}{4}$ hours

D $9\frac{1}{2}$ hours

E NH

13 Tamiko and her class helped plant 120 saplings at local parks on Earth Day. If 30 of the saplings were maple trees, what percent of the trees were maple trees?

F 90%

G 75%

H 25%

J $33\frac{1}{3}\%$

K NH

14 Molly bought 6 pounds of cornmeal at 39¢ per pound. How much did she spend on the cornmeal?

_____

_____

_____

_____

STOP

UNIT 7

LANGUAGE

PREWRITING, COMPOSING, AND EDITING

Directions: Read each sentence carefully. Then darken the circle for the correct answer to each question.

 TRY THIS Pretend that you are writing each sentence. Use the rules that you have learned for capitalization, punctuation, word usage, and sentence structure to choose the correct answer.

A Vacation on a Working Ranch

Celina and her family want to spend their vacation at a working ranch. Celina is trying to find more information about working ranches. She decides to write a letter to one of the ranches.

Sample A

Dear Director,
    I am writing to ask you to send me information about vacationing at your working ranch. My family and I such a vacation. Please send the information as soon as possible. We are anxious to plan our vacation.

Which of these is *not* a complete sentence?

A   I am writing to ask you to send me information about vacationing at your working ranch.

B   My family and I such a vacation.

C   Please send the information as soon as possible.

D   We are anxious to plan our vacation.

 THINK IT THROUGH The correct answer is <u>B</u>. <u>My family and I such a vacation</u> is not a complete sentence.

🛑 STOP

Writing a Research Paper

Ken is studying coral reefs in geography class. He is interested in learning more about the Great Barrier Reef along the northeast coast of Australia. Ken decides to use the Great Barrier Reef as the subject of his research paper for geography class.

1   Once Ken decides what to include in his research paper, what can he do to organize his paper?

A   plan a trip to the Great Barrier Reef

B   ask people what they know about coral reefs

C   make an outline or web of the information to include in the paper

D   determine the length of the paper

GO ON ➡

Answers
SA Ⓐ Ⓑ Ⓒ Ⓓ
1 Ⓐ Ⓑ Ⓒ Ⓓ

85

Ken found a book in the library on the Great Barrier Reef. Use the Table of Contents and Index from the book to answer questions 2–6.

Table of Contents

Index

2 Ken can find information in Chapter 1 about all of the following *except*—

F Australia

G cyclones

H colors of corals

J breakwater

3 Which pages would help Ken learn about Captain Cook's discovery of Australia?

A 13–17

B 48–49

C 57–61

D 21, 24

4 Which pages would have information about the types of coral found in the Great Barrier Reef?

F 1–6

G 21, 22

H 25

J 57–61

5 On which pages would Ken find information about caves found in the Great Barrier Reef?

A 18, 23, 35

B 21, 22

C 9, 11, 12

D 58–60

Write your answer for the following question:

6 Which chapter would have information about the kinds of fish that inhabit the Great Barrier Reef?

_____

_____

_____

_____

_____

_____

GO ON ➡

Answers

2 Ⓕ Ⓖ Ⓗ Ⓙ   **3** Ⓐ Ⓑ Ⓒ Ⓓ   **4** Ⓕ Ⓖ Ⓗ Ⓙ   **5** Ⓐ Ⓑ Ⓒ Ⓓ

Here is a rough draft of the first part of Ken's paper. Read the rough draft carefully. Then answer questions 7–12.

The Great Barrier Reef

(1) The Great Barrier Reef forms the largest reef on earth. (2) It is 1,250 miles long and is made up of the hardened skeletons of millions of dead water animals called coral polyps. (3) The Great Barrier Reef located in the South Pacific Ocean. (4) It lies along the northeast coast of Australia. (5) The reef contains a system of deep channels, lagoons, shallow pools, underwater caves, and ledges. (6) The Great Barrier Reef forms a breakwater, or wall, against the ocean. (7) The reef is constantly battered by ocean waves.

(8) Billions of living coral polyps make their home on the reef. (9) Some of these sea creatures are as big as a dime others are as tiny as a pinhead. (10) Their brilliant colors include green, yellow, blue, red, and purple. (11) Coral takes calcium from the ocean, changes it into lime, and uses the lime to construct its home on top of the dead coral. (12) I was impressed with the quality and taste of the fish. (13) In this home the coral remains for life.

(14) In 1770, Captain James Cook was the first person to lead an expedition to explore the Great Barrier Reef. (15) He was the captain of the ship *Endeavor;* and, perhaps, he was its navigator. (16) This flat-bottomed wooden ship was 106 feet long and 29 feet wide. (17) Cook and his crew explored the coast of Australia.

GO ON

7 Which group of words is *not* a complete sentence?

F 1

G 2

H 3

J 4

8 Which is the topic sentence of the second paragraph?

A 8

B 9

C 10

D 11

9 Which sentence could be added after sentence 7?

F Captain James Cook explored many islands in the Pacific Ocean.

G The reef is sturdy, however, providing a home to thousands of sea creatures.

H Barracuda can be seen hunting herring in the lagoons.

J The colorful coral is harvested for jewelry.

10 Which sentence does not belong in Ken's paper?

A 9

B 10

C 11

D 12

11 In sentence 15, the word *perhaps* does not appropriately connect the ideas. Which word or words should be used instead?

F however

G then

H thirdly

J in addition

12 Rewrite sentence 13 making the idea clearer.

_____

_____

_____

_____

_____

_____

_____

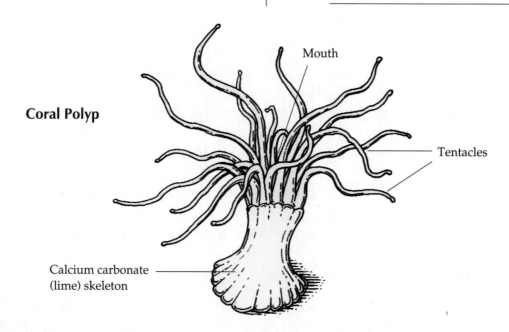

Coral Polyp

Mouth

Tentacles

Calcium carbonate (lime) skeleton

GO ON ▶

Here is the next part of Ken's rough draft for his paper. This part has certain words and phrases underlined. Read the draft carefully. Then answer questions 13–20.

Life is dangerous for the sea creatures of the Great Barrier Reef.
(18)

Most need protection from predators, or creatures that kill other
(19)

animals for food. Many animals are able to survived because their
(20)

colors or patterns camouflage them. For example, some brightly colored
(21)

fish live among the brightly colored corals and blend in with their

surroundings. Other fish change colors to match their surroundings.
(22)

Octopi are able to change their colors instantly. She can change quickly
(23)   (24)

from brown to blue to white to green to red to purple to stripes!

Lagoons, shallow ponds with no place to hide are dangerous places
(25)

for colorful fish. The bright colors of these fish would make it easy for
(26)

predators to see them. Therefore, fish that live in lagoons have dull
(27)

colors for protection.

The sea creatures of Australia's famous Reef have other ways of
(28)

protecting themselves from predators. For example, sea urchins have
(29)

long spines. They use these spines to prick or poison they predators. Sea
(30)   (31)

urchins also use the spines to secure their position in openings in coral.

A small sea slug, or nudibranch has no shell. It protects itself from
(32)   (33)

predators, by using poison. However, it doesn't produce its own poison.
(34)

Instead, this sea slug eats the poisonous parts of another sea creature,
(35)

the sea anemone. The sea slug can also sting predators with its tentacles.
(36)

GO ON

13 In sentence 18, <u>Life is dangerous</u> is best written—

    A Life was dangerous

    B Life are dangerous

    C Life were dangerous

    D As it is written.

14 In sentence 20, <u>survived</u> is best written—

    F has survived

    G survive

    H have survived

    J As it is written.

15 In sentence 24, <u>She can change</u> is best written—

    A They can change

    B He can change

    C We can change

    D As it is written.

16 Correctly rewrite sentence 25, <u>Lagoons, shallow ponds with no place to hide are dangerous places for colorful fish.</u>

_____

_____

_____

_____

_____

17 In sentence 28, <u>Australia's famous Reef</u> is best written—

    F australia's famous reef

    G Australia's famous reef

    H Australia's Famous Reef

    J As it is written.

18 In sentence 30, <u>poison they predators</u> is best written—

    A poison our predators

    B poison his predators

    C poison their predators

    D As it is written.

19 In sentence 32, <u>small sea slug, or nudibranch</u> is best written—

    F small sea slug or nudibranch

    G small, sea, slug or nudibranch

    H small sea slug, or nudibranch,

    J As it is written.

20 Correctly rewrite sentence 33, <u>It protects itself from predators, by using poison.</u>

_____

_____

_____

_____

_____

STOP

Answers
13 Ⓐ Ⓑ Ⓒ Ⓓ   **15** Ⓐ Ⓑ Ⓒ Ⓓ   **18** Ⓐ Ⓑ Ⓒ Ⓓ
90   **14** Ⓕ Ⓖ Ⓗ Ⓙ   **17** Ⓕ Ⓖ Ⓗ Ⓙ   **19** Ⓕ Ⓖ Ⓗ Ⓙ

Directions: Read each sentence carefully. If one of the words is misspelled, darken the circle for that word. If all the words are spelled correctly, then darken the circle for *No mistake*.

TRY THIS

Read each sentence carefully. If you are not sure of an answer, first decide which answer choices are spelled correctly. Then see if you can recognize the misspelled word from your reading experience.

Sample A

We were <u>planning</u> to get <u>something</u> to eat at <u>intramission</u>. <u>No mistake</u>
     A   B   C   D

THINK IT THROUGH

The correct answer is <u>C</u>. The prefix should be <u>inter</u>–, not <u>intra</u>–. The correct spelling is i-n-t-e-r-m-i-s-s-i-o-n.

STOP

1 The two groups <u>reached</u> a <u>compromise</u> after a week of <u>discussion</u>. <u>No mistake</u>
        A   B   C   D

2 Mr. McDonough will <u>announce</u> his <u>candidatcy</u> at a press <u>conference</u> next Friday. <u>No mistake</u>
        F   G   H   J

3 We <u>purifyed</u> the water with an <u>iodine</u> <u>tablet</u>. <u>No mistake</u>
   A   B C   D

4 Toshi's quick <u>reaction</u> <u>avertted</u> a potential <u>accident</u>. <u>No mistake</u>
       F   G   H   J

5 I am <u>doutful</u> that we will <u>arrive</u> in time for <u>dinner</u>. <u>No mistake</u>
    A   B   C   D

6 The loud music <u>coming</u> from next door <u>intrafered</u> with my <u>concentration</u>. <u>No mistake</u>
       F   G   H   J

7 The puppy was <u>wimpering</u> <u>outside</u> the door when she <u>arrived</u> home. <u>No mistake</u>
        A   B   C   D

8 The <u>souls</u> of my boots <u>need</u> to be <u>replaced</u>. <u>No mistake</u>
   F   G   H   J

STOP

Answers
SA Ⓐ Ⓑ Ⓒ Ⓓ   2 Ⓕ Ⓖ Ⓗ Ⓙ   4 Ⓕ Ⓖ Ⓗ Ⓙ   6 Ⓕ Ⓖ Ⓗ Ⓙ   8 Ⓕ Ⓖ Ⓗ Ⓙ
1 Ⓐ Ⓑ Ⓒ Ⓓ   3 Ⓐ Ⓑ Ⓒ Ⓓ   5 Ⓐ Ⓑ Ⓒ Ⓓ   7 Ⓐ Ⓑ Ⓒ Ⓓ

Sample A

> The world's first public railroad opened
> **(1)**
> in England in 1825. It operated between
> **(2)**
> the towns of Stockton and Darlington, a
>
> distance of 20 miles.
>
> By 1830 railways were operating in
> **(3)**
> France, Germany, Canada, Spain and,
>
> Switzerland.

How is sentence 3 best written?

A By 1830 railways were operating in France and Germany, Canada, Spain and Switzerland.

B By 1830 railways were operating in, France, Germany, Canada, Spain, and Switzerland.

C By 1830 railways were operating in France, Germany, Canada, Spain, and Switzerland.

D As it is written.

STOP

The Olympic Games

Carl hopes to attend the next summer Olympic Games. Carl decides to write a letter to the United States Olympic Committee to learn more about the Olympics.

1 Carl wants to find books about the history of the Olympic Games. Which kind of card catalog will best help him find a book about the Olympic Games?

A Title

B Author

C Bibliography

D Subject

2 Why is Carl writing a letter to the United States Olympic Committee?

_____

_____

_____

_____

_____

_____

Carl used a dictionary to look up some words he wants to use in his letter to the United States Olympic Committee. Use the dictionary entry and the Pronunciation Guide to answer questions 3 and 4.

> **pen•tath•lon** [pen tath′ lən] n. An athletic contest that features each athlete participating in five different events.

> **Pronunciation Guide**
>
> at; āpe; fär; câre; end; mē; it; īce; pîerce; hot; ōld; sông; fôrk; oil; out; up; ūse; rüle; púll; tûrn; chin; sing; shop; thin; this; hw in white; zh in treasure. The symbol ə stands for the unstressed vowel sound in about, taken, pencil, lemon, and circus.

3 What is the correct way to divide pentathlon into syllables?

F pen ta thlon   **H** pent a thlon

G pen tath lon   **J** pent ath lon

4 The "a" in pentathlon sounds most like the vowel sound in—

A handkerchief

B negative

C partnership

D everyday

GO ON

Answers
SA Ⓐ Ⓑ Ⓒ Ⓓ   1 Ⓐ Ⓑ Ⓒ Ⓓ   3 Ⓕ Ⓖ Ⓗ Ⓙ   4 Ⓐ Ⓑ Ⓒ Ⓓ

Here is a rough draft of the first part of Carl's letter. Read the rough draft carefully. Then answer questions 5 and 6.

Dear U.S. Olympic Committee Members,

I am an enthusiastic fan of the Olympic Games! I especially enjoy, the
(1)   (2)
events in the Summer Games. I am writing for more information about
(3)
the Olympics.

I know the Olympic Games consist of the Summer Games and the
(4)
Winter Games. How is it decided where the games will be held? What
(5)   (6)
events are held in the Summer Games, and what are held in the

Winter Games?

I never miss the opening ceremonies of each Olympic Game. The
(7)   (8)
lighting of the Olympic Flame is awesome! I've read that the lighted
(9)
torch is brought from the valley of Olympia, Greece, by cross-country

runners. My aunt lived in Greece for a year. What other traditions are
(10)   (11)
practiced at the opening ceremonies of the Olympic Games?

---

5   What is the best way to write sentence 2?

F   I especially, enjoy the events in the Summer Games.

G   I, especially, enjoy the events in the summer games.

H   I especially enjoy the events in the Summer Games.

J   As it is written.

6   Which sentence does *not* belong in this letter? Write the number.

_____

_____

_____

_____

_____

GO ON ➡

Answers
5 Ⓕ Ⓖ Ⓗ Ⓙ

Here is the next part of Carl's rough draft for his letter. This part has certain words and phrases underlined. Read the draft carefully. Then answer questions 7–12.

I have read that an Olympic athlete must be a citizen of the sponsor country.
(12)

Does an athlete actually have to live in the country <u>they represent</u>?
(13)

<u>Starting with the 1988 Olympics</u> professional athletes were allowed to compete.
(14)

National Olympic committees are allowed to <u>pay our athletes</u> while they train
(15)

for the Olympics. How much money does the United States Olympic Committee
(16)

pay athletes?

In <u>"Modern Olympic Games the fifth</u> chapter of *A History of the Olympics*, I
(17)

read that each country is allowed to use its own method for selecting athletes for

the Games. To be chosen from the United States, an athlete must finish high in
(18)

the competitions. Will this method of selection ever change?
(19)

How are Olympic events judged? I know that <u>in diving, figure skating, and
(20)   (21)

<u>gymnastics</u> events, medalists are chosen by judges based on points awarded for

their performances. How are medalists chosen in swimming and track events?
(22)

I have one last question. Is it true that the Olympic Games were canceled
(23)   (24)

during <u>world Wars I and II</u>?

I look forward to receiving answers to my questions. I appreciate your time
(25)   (26)

and attention.

Sincerely yours,
Carl Hafner

GO ON

7 In sentence 13, <u>they represent?</u> is best written—

   A he or she represents?

   B you represent?

   C we represent?

   D As it is written.

8 In sentence 14, <u>Starting with the 1988 Olympics</u> is best written—

   F Starting with the 1988, Olympics

   G Starting with the 1988 Olympics,

   H Starting, with the 1988 Olympics

   J As it is written.

9 What word should be substituted for "our" in sentence 15, <u>pay our athletes?</u>

   _____

   _____

   _____

   _____

   _____

10 Correctly rewrite sentence 17, "<u>Modern Olympic Games the fifth</u>—

   A "Modern Olympic Games," the fifth

   B Modern Olympic Games the fifth

   C "Modern Olympic" Games the fifth

   D As it is written.

11 In sentence 21, <u>in diving, figure skating, and gymnastics</u> is best written—

   F in diving, figure, skating, and gymnastics

   G in diving figure skating and gymnastics

   H in diving, figure skating and, gymnastics

   J As it is written.

12 In sentence 24, <u>world Wars I and II?</u> is best written—

   A world war one and two?

   B World war I and II?

   C World Wars I and II?

   D As it is written.

GO ON ➡

Answers

7 Ⓐ Ⓑ Ⓒ Ⓓ   **8** Ⓕ Ⓖ Ⓗ Ⓙ   **10** Ⓐ Ⓑ Ⓒ Ⓓ   **11** Ⓕ Ⓖ Ⓗ Ⓙ   **12** Ⓐ Ⓑ Ⓒ Ⓓ

For questions 13–24, read each sentence carefully. If one of the words is misspelled, darken the circle for that word. If all the words are spelled correctly, then darken the circle for *No mistake*.

13 Dr. Rivera <u>treats</u> a number of <u>patience</u> at the West Side <u>Clinic</u>. <u>No mistake</u>
     F   G   H   J

14 The <u>pressure</u> <u>intensifyed</u> as the gymnastics competition moved into the final <u>stages</u>. <u>No mistake</u>
     A   B   C   D

15 The <u>winning</u> rose at the <u>annual</u> garden show has a <u>suttle</u> fragrance. <u>No mistake</u>
     F   G   H   J

16 The <u>manager</u> gave us <u>complementary</u> tickets to the next matinee. <u>No mistake</u>
     A   B   C   D

17 Mary <u>canceled</u> her <u>reservation</u> when she <u>herd</u> the news. <u>No mistake</u>
       F   G   H   J

18 Beautiful <u>frescoes</u> <u>adorned</u> the walls of the <u>ancient</u> temple. <u>No mistake</u>
            A   B   C   D

19 <u>Literatcy</u> <u>continues</u> to be an important <u>issue</u> in our country. <u>No mistake</u>
     F   G   H   J

20 The United Nations is a <u>truly</u> <u>intranational</u> <u>organization</u>. <u>No mistake</u>
                        A   B   C   D

21 The <u>seem</u> on my shirt <u>started</u> to <u>unravel</u>. <u>No mistake</u>
       F   G   H   J

22 The American team <u>prevailled</u> over the German team in the <u>volleyball</u> <u>match</u>. <u>No mistake</u>
                    A   B   C   D

23 Reynaldo was a <u>talented</u> <u>amateur</u> tennis <u>player</u>. <u>No mistake</u>
            F   G   H   J

24 My <u>grandfather</u> liked to sit on the <u>porch</u> swing in the evening and <u>wittle</u>. <u>No mistake</u>
        A   B   C   D

STOP

Answers

13 Ⓕ Ⓖ Ⓗ Ⓙ	16 Ⓐ Ⓑ Ⓒ Ⓓ	19 Ⓕ Ⓖ Ⓗ Ⓙ	22 Ⓐ Ⓑ Ⓒ Ⓓ
14 Ⓐ Ⓑ Ⓒ Ⓓ	17 Ⓕ Ⓖ Ⓗ Ⓙ	20 Ⓐ Ⓑ Ⓒ Ⓓ	23 Ⓕ Ⓖ Ⓗ Ⓙ
15 Ⓕ Ⓖ Ⓗ Ⓙ	18 Ⓐ Ⓑ Ⓒ Ⓓ	21 Ⓕ Ⓖ Ⓗ Ⓙ	24 Ⓐ Ⓑ Ⓒ Ⓓ

READING COMPREHENSION

Use the removable answer sheet on page 127 to record your answers for the practice tests.

Sample A
Cliff Dwellings

Mesa Verde National Park is located in southwestern Colorado and has some of the most astounding cliff dwellings found in the United States. Approximately eight hundred years ago, the Anasazi people used stone blocks to construct apartment-like dwellings in the caves of the canyon walls.

Which of these is a *fact* stated in the selection?

A The cliff dwellings have lasted because they were built well.

B The cliff dwellings were never completed.

C The Anasazi should have built with brick.

D The Anasazi cliff dwellings were like apartments.

STOP

For questions 1–33, carefully read each selection and the questions that follow. Darken the circle for the correct answer, or write in your answer.

Chicago

Skyscrapers tower
along Lake Michigan
like building blocks.

They seem to lean
toward one another
as if for support.

In their glass sides we see
a reflection in primary colors
of sunset, water, and parks.

Unknowing, they take in
their surroundings and return them
to us as a dream.

1   **The poem compares the reflection from the skyscrapers' glass sides to—**

A real life.

B a dream.

C a subconscious desire.

D an artist's inspiration.

2   **This poem was probably written to describe—**

F how Chicago's skyscrapers look.

G how Chicago is not a dream.

H a sunset on Lake Michigan.

J buildings that look like they are dreaming.

3   **The buildings are compared to—**

A sunsets.

B blocks.

C parks.

D glass.

GO ON

Recycling Plastics

The best way to solve the problem of throw-away plastics is to find practical ways to reuse them. Many useful things are being made from recycled plastics. There are more than fifty types of plastics in use. They are made using a variety of chemicals, dyes, and processes. The different properties of plastics make them suitable for different types of recycled products. The chart below shows the types of plastic products used to recycle into new products. The six codes allow recyclers to separate plastics into groups of types that have the same properties.

PLASTICS RECYCLING CHART

Symbol	Uses	Recycled Products (made from recyclable plastics)
1 PETE	Plastic soft drink bottles, mouthwash jars, peanut butter and salad dressing bottles	Liquid soap bottles, strapping, fiberfill for winter coats, surfboards, paintbrushes, fuzz on tennis balls, soft drink bottles, film, egg cartons, skis, carpets, boats
2 HDPE	Milk, water, and juice containers; grocery bags; toys; liquid detergent bottles	Soft drink bottle base cups, flowerpots, drain pipes, signs, stadium seats, trash cans, recycling bins, traffic-barrier cones, golf bag liners, detergent bottles, toys
3 V	Clear food packaging, shampoo bottles	Floor mats, pipes, hose, mud flaps
4 LDPE	Bread bags, frozen food bags, grocery bags	Garbage bag liners, grocery bags, multipurpose bags
5 PP	Ketchup bottles, yogurt containers and margarine tubs, medicine bottles	Manhole steps, paint buckets, videocassette storage cases, ice scrapers, fast food trays, lawn mower wheels, automobile battery parts
6 PS	Videocassette cases, compact disk jackets, coffee cups, knives, spoons, forks, cafeteria trays, grocery meat trays, fast food sandwich containers	License plate holders, golf course and septic tank drainage systems, desktop accessories, hanging files, food service trays, flower pots, trash cans, videocassettes

GO ON ➤

4   What is the code symbol for plastic products that can be recycled into hose?

F   PP

G   V

H   HDPE

J   PS

5   What is the correct code number for such products as bread bags and grocery bags?

A   1

B   3

C   4

D   5

6   What is the purpose of the symbols on plastic products?

F   to make it easy for recyclers to sort plastics

G   to indicate to consumers what new products will be made from the product

H   to indicate to scientists the properties of the product

J   to indicate to stores how much to charge for the product

7   Which of the following shows an original product and its recyclable product?

A   peanut butter jars into mud flaps

B   detergent bottles into grocery bags

C   bread bags into surfboards

D   medicine bottles into ice scrapers

8   List three recyclable products that can be made from videocassette cases and compact disk jackets.

_____

_____

_____

_____

_____

9   If you wanted to learn more about recycling plastics, which of the following articles would you choose to read?

F   "Solving the Solid Waste Problem"

G   "The History of Durable Goods"

H   "Plastic Surgery Success Stories"

J   "Manufacturing Plastics"

10 If the author added a sentence to the end of the introduction, which of these would best fit?

A   Plastic "wood" never rots or splinters or gets termites.

B   Then the plastics, grouped by code, can be shipped to companies that recycle plastics.

C   Plastics are strong and used for thousands of purposes.

D   Too many plastic products are disposed of immediately after using them just once.

11 Which code symbol is used for original plastic products that can be turned into recyclable plastic products such as skis, egg cartons, and film?

_____

_____

_____

_____

GO ON

The Magic Tapestry: A Chinese Folktale

Long ago a widow lived in a cottage with her three sons. She supported the family by weaving tapestries. The tapestries were exquisite works of art that sold for much gold. One day the widow started a new tapestry. She wove into her fabric a magnificent mansion surrounded by brilliant flower gardens. Receding into the distance were rolling hills and towering mountains. Every day for months the widow worked on the tapestry. With *painstaking* care she added intricate details. She created a babbling brook with exotic fish, then wove a graceful footbridge.

Meanwhile Li Mo, her eldest son, and Li Tu, her middle son, began complaining. "When are you going to finish? We have no rice, and our clothes are ragged," Li Mo said. "Hurry and finish so that we can sell the tapestry," Li Tu demanded.

But their mother said nothing. She continued working at the loom from sunrise until late at night. Li Ju, her youngest son, became a woodcutter so that the family could eat.

One day after toiling for more than a year, the widow announced that the tapestry was almost complete. As Li Ju watched, she wove a resemblance of herself into the wall hanging. "This must be your dream," Li Ju said with conviction. The widow wove Li Ju's image into the work.

The other two brothers came in and tried to pry the tapestry off the loom. But their mother wouldn't let them touch it. She said, "This is a picture of everything I wish for and cherish. All my children should be in it, but I haven't had time to weave you in."

"What does it matter? Just give it to us so that we can sell it," Li Mo said. "Yes, all we care about is the gold," Li Tu added cruelly.

Just then a tremendous wind ripped the tapestry from the loom. The treasured work flew out the window and vanished into the eastern sky. The family raced outside but could not *retrieve* it. The widow was devastated. She called Li Mo and told him to travel east in search of the tapestry. "If you don't find it, I will surely die," she said.

Li Mo traveled east for a month; then he came to an old woman who lived in a stone hut. Outside the hut was a stone stallion. The woman told Li Mo that the fairies of Sun Mountain had stolen the tapestry. She said that Li Mo should pierce his finger and bleed on the stone horse. The stallion would take him to Sun Mountain. The old woman described the fiery mountains and icy seas he would have to cross on his journey. Li Mo shuddered at the thought of blood, fire, and ice. But when the old woman offered him a choice between the journey and a bag of gold, he gladly took the gold and traveled to the big city, forgetting about the tapestry.

The widow was becoming weaker. When Li Mo did not return she sent Li Tu. But when Li Tu met the old woman in the hut he also accepted the gold and went to the big city. Li Ju pleaded with his mother to let him search for the tapestry. He knew that his mother was very ill.

When Li Ju reached the stone hut, he eagerly listened to the old woman's instructions. When she offered him a bag of gold, he refused. "I must find the tapestry or my mother will die," he said. Courageously he galloped through the fires and over the icy seas. At last he arrived at Sun Mountain. He was greeted by a beautiful fairy dressed in crimson. The fairy said that she would return the tapestry. The next morning she folded it and handed it to Li Ju. She bid him farewell, and Li Ju journeyed homeward. He hurried because he knew his mother must be near death. Finally he arrived and hung the tapestry on the wall so that his mother could see it. Magically the tapestry expanded until it became a giant landscape. Mother and son walked into the peaceful scene. Waiting for them at the door of the mansion was the fairy dressed in crimson. Li Ju married the fairy, and the three of them lived contentedly on the lovely estate.

One day two beggars who were really Li Mo and Li Tu knocked at the iron gate of the mansion. But a ferocious windstorm carried them away and deposited them on a desolate road. Each beggar held a tattered piece of tapestry in his hands.

GO ON➡

12 Where does this story take place?

    F in Japan

    G in China

    H in India

    J in Thailand

13 The widow supported her family by—

    A cutting wood.

    B selling weaving equipment.

    C weaving beautiful tapestries.

    D sewing clothes for rich people.

14 In this story, *painstaking* means—

    F causing intense pain.

    G great speed.

    H over and over again.

    J careful and diligent.

15 By complaining about the time that their mother spent on the tapestry, Li Mo and Li Tu show that—

    A they are worried about their mother's health.

    B they are anxious to learn how to weave.

    C they are concerned only about themselves.

    D they dislike the tapestry.

16 Why did the widow work so long and hard on the new tapestry?

_____

_____

_____

_____

_____

_____

17 Li Mo and Li Tu were beggars because—

    F they could not find steady work.

    G they had been fired from their jobs.

    H they were sick and could not find work.

    J they had spent all their gold in the city and were too lazy to work.

18 In this story, the word *retrieve* means—

    A sell.

    B throw.

    C get back.

    D return.

19 Why were Li Mo and Li Tu swept by a ferocious windstorm?

    F They were being punished.

    G They were in the wrong place at the wrong time.

    H It was the windy season.

    J The fairy wanted them to go to Sun Mountain.

20 What lessons can be learned from this story?

_____

_____

_____

_____

_____

_____

_____

_____

GO ON ➡

A Great American Patriot

Paul Revere was made famous by the poet Henry Wadsworth Longfellow in the poem "Paul Revere's Ride." Other details of Revere's life are less well-known, but probably as important to the effort to free the American colonies from British rule.

Revere was born in 1735 in Boston, Massachusetts, and was of French descent. His father was a silversmith, which is why Revere learned that trade while he also studied at Boston's North Grammar School.

Revere's work as the leader of the Boston craftworkers fired his interest in freedom for the American colonies. He worked alongside Samuel Adams and John Hancock—two revolutionary leaders. Revere was a *co-conspirator* in the Boston Tea Party. He created engravings of political cartoons in support of American liberty. He often delivered special messages to Boston patriots.

During the Revolutionary War, Paul Revere commanded a unit at Castle William in Boston Harbor. He later led the artillery division in a failed attempt to recapture control of land in Maine. *Accusations* of cowardice and disobedience were filed against Revere in connection with this failed attempt. He was found not guilty at his court-martial and later left the service.

Revere's other contributions to the Revolutionary War effort included the manufacture of gunpowder for the Continental Army, the designing and printing of the Continental currency, and the creation of the state seal that is still used by Massachusetts. In addition, Revere's knowledge of metal working was helpful when he made bronze cannons for the army.

Revere's silversmithing trade continued after the war. His silver tea sets are prized possessions for those fortunate enough to own them. He also cast bronze bells, which are still used in parts of New England today. His skill was put to good use when he made the copper fittings for the warship *U.S.S. Constitution*, also known as *Old Ironsides*.

GO ON ➡

21 Why did Paul Revere learn the trade of silversmithing?

   A He learned the trade at Boston's North Grammar School.

   B He wanted to work with Samuel Adams.

   C His father was a silversmith.

   D He wanted to make copper fittings for warships.

22 What is the third paragraph *mainly* about?

   F Paul Revere's military career

   G Paul Revere's work in the American colonies' fight for freedom

   H Paul Revere's work as a silversmith

   J Paul Revere's education

23 In this selection, *co-conspirator* means—

   A one of many who were arrested.

   B a famous society person.

   C part owner.

   D one who secretly plots with others.

24 Which of Paul Revere's contributions to the Revolutionary War effort is the most famous?

   F the manufacture of gunpowder for the Continental Army

   G the design and printing of the Continental currency

   H his engravings of political cartoons

   J his ride to warn the American colonists that the British were coming

25 In this selection, the word *accusations* means—

   A formal charges.

   B proven lies.

   C military honors.

   D idle rumors.

26 There is enough information in this article to show that—

   F Paul Revere contributed in many ways to American freedom.

   G Paul Revere was the best soldier during the Revolutionary War.

   H Paul Revere was an excellent student at Boston's North Grammar School.

   J Paul Revere was a disappointing silversmith.

27 The web shows some ideas discussed in the selection.

What word(s) would go in the empty box?

_____

_____

_____

_____

_____

_____

_____

_____

GO ON➡

SPEEDAWAY

The only name in bicycles

Our bicycles are the fastest ones on the road. That's why
SPEEDAWAY is the bicycle brand you know and trust.

We make our bicycles with the customer in mind. Each bicycle is a
SUPERIOR machine. You can't buy anything better. We guarantee
that this bicycle will not be the CHEAPEST one you can buy.
But we do guarantee that it is the BEST brand you can buy.

Our bicycles offer many special features. Here are some of them:

- 21 speeds

- Light-touch gearshifts for easy and accurate shifting

- Hand-pull caliper brakes

- 2-inch white sidewall tires

- Gel-filled, cushioned seat

- 26-inch aluminum frame—This NEW and IMPROVED frame combines
  a reliably sturdy frame with the weight of a feather to produce a bicycle
  that seems to fly down the road.

- 5-function electronic trip-monitor that displays: speed, distance, average
  speed per mile, calories burned per mile, and length of time.

We truly believe in our bicycles. We are so sure you will like our bicycles
that we will give you THREE FREE GIFTS—a safety helmet, a water
bottle, and a pouch bag—when you purchase a SPEEDAWAY bicycle.
If you are not satisfied with your bicycle, you may return it for your money
back. BUT YOU GET TO KEEP THE FREE GIFTS!

Hurry on down to your local sporting goods store. If they don't have this
bicycle, it's because they're sold out! Everyone carries our brand.

Buy SPEEDAWAY! You'll thank yourself for many years to come.

GO ON ➡

28 Which of these is an *opinion* in the ad?

    A You can't buy anything better…

    B …electronic trip-monitor that displays: speed, distance, …

    C …you may return it for your money back…

    D …you get to keep the free gifts…

29 All of these are features of the Speedaway bicycle *except*—

    F 2-inch white-wall tires.

    G a see-through plastic bug shield.

    H hand-pull caliper brakes.

    J a gel-filled cushioned seat.

30 There is enough information in the ad to show that this product is—

    A made in the United States.

    B sold in most sporting goods stores.

    C the poorest-selling bicycle in the country.

    D used by most professional sports stars.

31 This ad was written mainly to tell about—

    F the many products made by the manufacturers of the Speedaway brand bicycle.

    G a new invention that is being sold.

    H the many features of a brand-name bicycle.

    J the stores where you can buy bicycles.

32 The ad tries to appeal to your desire to—

    A buy a brand-name bicycle.

    B have a bicycle like your best friend's bicycle.

    C spend less money.

    D look good.

33 The ad states that if you are not satisfied with the bicycle you may return it, get your money back, and keep the free gifts. Why do you think the company is making this offer?

_____

_____

_____

_____

_____

_____

_____

PRACTICE TEST 2

READING VOCABULARY

Sample A

Something that is <u>desolate</u> is—

A happy

B bright

C bleak

D colorful

STOP

For questions 1–8, darken the circle for the word or group of words that has the same or almost the same meaning as the underlined word.

1 <u>Sequence</u> means—

A one at a time

B all at once

C in order

D as a group

2 <u>Puny</u> means—

F large

G significant

H tiny

J attractive

3 To <u>confirm</u> is to—

A believe

B contain

C choose

D prove

4 To <u>attain</u> something is to—

F lose it

G achieve it

H fail it

J confuse it

5 A <u>cunning</u> person is—

A popular

B sly

C educated

D well-known

6 Someone who is <u>fashionable</u> is—

F outdated

G clumsy

H crude

J stylish

7 A <u>smirk</u> is a kind of—

A smile

B cloth

C sound

D insult

8 Something that is <u>severe</u> is—

F weak

G harsh

H complete

J empty

GO ON

Sample B

> Mom asked Tom to load the groceries into the car.

In which sentence does load have the same meaning as it does in the sentence above?

A The mule carried a heavy load.

B Her letter took a load off my mind.

C Did you load the film into the camera?

D We drove the load of potatoes to market.

For questions 9–13, darken the circle for the sentence in which the underlined word means the same as it does in the sentence in the box.

9
> The old prospector found a gold mine.

In which sentence does mine have the same meaning as it does in the sentence above?

A The library is a mine of information.

B Is this sweater yours or mine?

C They own an agate mine.

D Do they mine harbors with explosives?

10
> I lost my ring near the tennis net.

In which sentence does net have the same meaning as it does in the sentence above?

F She will net the fish.

G The net weight of the package is 9 ounces.

H Grandma always wears a hair net to bed at night.

J Will he net any profits from his investments?

11
> The meteorologists will track the hurricane.

In which sentence does track have the same meaning as it does in the sentence above?

A What animal made this track?

B Jimmy was about to track mud on the new carpet.

C I was able to track the injured animal into the woods.

D Dr. Lee knows he's on the right track with his research.

12
> The Mississippi River is a major waterway.

In which sentence does major have the same meaning as it does in the sentence above?

F Is this symphony in a major key?

G My uncle held the army rank of major.

H I plan to major in science in college.

J Suzanne spends the major part of her time studying.

13
> Louisa will begin first grade in the fall.

In which sentence does grade have the same meaning as it does in the sentence above?

A What is the highest grade of beef?

B Kareem is now in the sixth grade.

C I will try to grade all your papers tonight.

D Renee has taken a grade six government job.

GO ON

Sample C

We tried to procure enough supplies to last for five days. Procure means—

A acquire

B pack

C find

D borrow

STOP

For questions 14–21, darken the circle for the word or words that give the meaning of the underlined word, or write in the answer.

14 My throat was parched after three hours in the sun. Parched means—

F sore

G red

H dry

J wet

15 The expert says that bowl is authentic Wedgwood china. Authentic means—

A ancient

B genuine

C false

D elegant

16 Janet did not care for his brash manner. Brash means—

F polite

G intelligent

H rude

J quiet

17 The flaw in the fabric made it unusable. Flaw means—

_____

_____

_____

_____

18 Many words are confusing because they have multiple meanings. Multiple means—

A individual

B few

C long

D several

19 The horde of aggressive reporters following the movie star was a big problem. Horde means—

F small group

G crowd

H few

J individual

20 Sandra said that she will strive to make the basketball team no matter how much work it takes. Strive means—

A try

B ask

C quit

D rest

21 Max was flabbergasted by the number of people who came to his birthday party. Flabbergasted means—

_____

_____

_____

_____

STOP

PART 1: MATH PROBLEM SOLVING

Sample A

Which fraction is greater than $\frac{5}{8}$?

A $\frac{2}{4}$ C $\frac{3}{4}$

B $\frac{2}{7}$ D $\frac{3}{5}$

STOP

For questions 1–47, darken the circle for the correct answer, or write in the answer.

1 Which of the following decimals is greater than 0.273 and less than 0.291?

  A   0.279

  B   0.295

  C   0.259

  D   0.209

2 The number line shows 4 mice in a race. Which mouse is in the lead?

  F   Mouse A

  G   Mouse B

  H   Mouse C

  J   Mouse D

3 The temperature reading was –15°C at sunrise. By 3:00 P.M., the temperature had risen 20°. What was the temperature then?

_____

_____

4 At the candy store, 4 children each grabbed a handful of wrapped candy from the candy bin. The candy cost $1.49 per pound. The first child's handful of candy weighed $\frac{1}{3}$ pound. The second child's handful weighed $\frac{2}{5}$ pound, the third child's weighed $\frac{3}{10}$ pound, and the fourth's weighed $\frac{1}{4}$ pound. Which shows these amounts arranged in order from largest to smallest?

  A $\frac{2}{5}, \frac{1}{3}, \frac{3}{10}, \frac{1}{4}$

  B $\frac{3}{10}, \frac{1}{4}, \frac{2}{5}, \frac{1}{3}$

  C $\frac{1}{4}, \frac{2}{5}, \frac{3}{10}, \frac{1}{3}$

  D $\frac{1}{3}, \frac{2}{5}, \frac{1}{4}, \frac{3}{10}$

5 Which of these temperatures is colder than the temperature shown on the thermometer?

  F   –6°

  G   –2°

  H   3°

  J   0°

6 In the jet-engine racing car *Spirit of America,* a person can travel at 613.995 miles per hour. What is the value of the 5 in this number?

  A   5 ten-thousandths

  B   5 thousandths

  C   5 hundredths

  D   5 tenths

GO ON ➡

7 Madelynn lives 3 times as far from school as Liz does. If x is the number of blocks that Liz lives from school, which expression represents the distance Madelynn lives from school?

F $3x$

G $x - 3$

H $x + 3$

J $x/3$

8 Each ▱ represents 0.03.

What decimal is shown by the figures above?

A 104

B 10.41

C 1.04

D 0.104

9 A special machine changes numbers according to a certain rule. The *out* number in the table shows the result when the rule is applied to the *in* number.

In	6	15	27
Out	2	5	9

What number will 24 be changed to ?

_____

_____

_____

_____

_____

10 Dexter does volunteer work at a local retirement village. He wants to take some of the residents to a movie. The tickets cost $4.00 each. Dexter figures that it will cost $6.00 to drive his van to and from the movie theater. Which expression can Dexter use to find C, the total cost of the outing?

F $C = 4 + 6 + n$

G $6n - 4 = C + 6$

H $C = 4n + 6$

J $6(4n) = C$

11 The Richter Scale measures the magnitude of earthquakes and ranks them on a scale of 1 to 10. Each number on the scale stands for 30 times the magnitude of the number just before it. For example, if a reading on the Richter Scale is 2 more than another quake, it is 30^2 times the magnitude. If an earthquake had a Richter Scale reading of 7, how would this be written to compare it to an earthquake with a Richter Scale reading of 2?

A 30^2

B 30^3

C 30^5

D 30^7

12 Look at the factor tree shown here.

Which numbers are missing from the factor tree?

F 2, 7

G 3, 6

H 4, 5

J 6, 9

GO ON➡

110

13 When 30 students were surveyed, 6 stated that they watch $2\frac{1}{2}$ hours of television each day. If 450 students were surveyed, how many students could be expected to watch $2\frac{1}{2}$ hours of television each day?

A 5

B 20

C 90

D 420

14 Cybil was making a design for art class by gluing beads to posterboard. She had 2 beads in the first row, 5 beads in the second row, 8 beads in the third row, and 11 beads in the fourth row. If this pattern continues, how many beads will she use in each of the next 3 rows?

F 22, 25, 28

G 12, 15, 18

H 15, 19, 23

J 14, 17, 20

15 If digits cannot be repeated, how many 3-digit numbers can be made using only the digits 3, 5, 6, 8, and 9?

A 5

B 24

C 36

D 60

16 What is another way to write $(4 \times 6) + (4 \times 4)$?

_____

_____

_____

_____

_____

_____

_____

17 Howard used an air pump to launch a model rocket. The table shows the number of pumps required to launch the rocket to specific heights. If it continued to operate at this rate, how many pumps would be required to launch the rocket to a height of at least 100 feet?

Number of Pumps	Height in Feet
3	40
4	47.5
5	55
6	62.5
7	70

F 12

G 11

H 10

J 8

18 Angela has only 6 nickels and 8 pennies in her coin purse. What is the probability that Angela will randomly pick a nickel out of her coin purse?

A $\frac{3}{7}$

B $\frac{1}{8}$

C $\frac{5}{5}$

D $\frac{1}{2}$

19 In how many different ways can the letters in the word *MATH* be arranged?

_____

_____

_____

_____

_____

_____

_____

GO ON ➡

Use the graph to answer questions 20–22.

Skate-Rite Monthly Sales

● Skateboards □ Skates

20 Which month on the graph shows the fewest sales of skateboards?

F January

G February

H September

J November

21 About how many more skates were sold in April than in November?

A 5,000

B 10,000

C 15,000

D 25,000

22 Describe the sale of skateboards between April and July.

_____

_____

_____

_____

In one week, a pet store made $1,000 in profits. The following graph shows the types of sales. Study the graph and answer questions 23 and 24.

PET STORE PROFITS

Total Profits = $1000

23 Which tally chart shows the data in the circle graph above?

F

Cats	⦀⦀ ⦀⦀ ⦀⦀ ⦀⦀
Dogs	⦀⦀ ⦀⦀ ⦀⦀
Fish	⦀⦀ ⦀⦀ ⦀⦀ ⦀⦀
Birds	⦀⦀ ⦀⦀ ⦀⦀
Other	⦀⦀ ⦀⦀

G

Cats	⦀⦀ ⦀⦀
Dogs	⦀⦀ ⦀⦀ ⦀⦀
Fish	⦀⦀ ⦀⦀ ⦀⦀ ⦀⦀ IIII
Birds	⦀⦀ ⦀⦀ ⦀⦀ I
Other	⦀⦀ ⦀⦀ II

H

Cats	⦀⦀ ⦀⦀ ⦀⦀ ⦀⦀
Dogs	⦀⦀ ⦀⦀ ⦀⦀ ⦀⦀ ⦀⦀ ⦀⦀
Fish	⦀⦀ ⦀⦀ ⦀⦀ ⦀⦀ IIII
Birds	⦀⦀ ⦀⦀ ⦀⦀ ⦀⦀
Other	⦀⦀

J

Cats	⦀⦀ ⦀⦀ ⦀⦀ ⦀⦀ II
Dogs	⦀⦀ ⦀⦀ ⦀⦀ II
Fish	⦀⦀ ⦀⦀ ⦀⦀ ⦀⦀ ⦀⦀ I
Birds	⦀⦀ ⦀⦀ ⦀⦀ III
Other	⦀⦀ III

24 How much more did the store make from sales of dogs than sales of cats?

_____

_____

GO ON➡

25 Which transformation moves the figure from position A to position B?

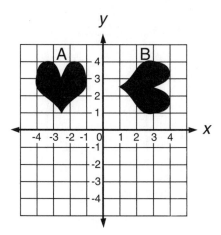

A extension

B rotation

C reflection

D translation

26 This bar graph shows Arnie's test scores in math class. What is his average (mean) score?

F 85

G 80

H 75

J 70

This table shows the prices and the number of shoes in stock in a shoe store. Study the table. Then answer questions 27 and 28.

Shoes in Stock		
Color	Number	Price per Pair
Red	54	$50
Brown	50	$35
Black	60	$36
Navy	46	$45

27 How many pairs of red shoes and navy shoes are in stock?

A 100

B 106

C 110

D 210

28 How much do 2 pairs of black shoes and 1 pair of navy shoes cost?

_____

_____

_____

_____

29 The diameter of circle J is represented by which line segment?

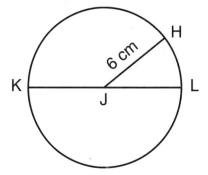

F $\overline{JH}$

G $\overline{JL}$

H $\overline{JK}$

J $\overline{KL}$

GO ON➡

30 Which coordinates best represent the location of Banner on the map?

A (4, 1)

B (3, 2)

C (2, 1)

D (2, 3)

31 Which angle shown here is an acute angle?

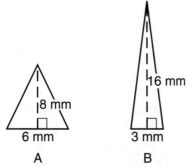

Use the two triangles shown here to answer question 32.

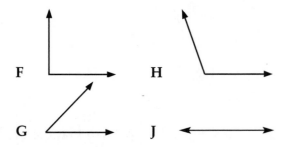

32 Which of the following statements about the two triangles is true?

A Triangle A is smaller in area than Triangle B.

B Both Triangle A and Triangle B have six angles that are right angles.

C The area of Triangle A is one-third larger than that of Triangle B.

D The area of Triangle A is equal to the area of Triangle B.

33 If each cube shown here represents 1 cubic unit, what is the volume of this figure?

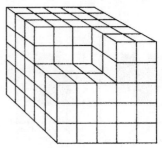

F 125 cubic units

G 113 cubic units

H 105 cubic units

J 25 cubic units

34 Each of the figures shown here can be folded to form a three-dimensional figure. Which can be folded to form a cube?

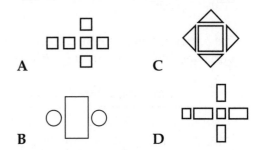

35 Which lines shown here are parallel?

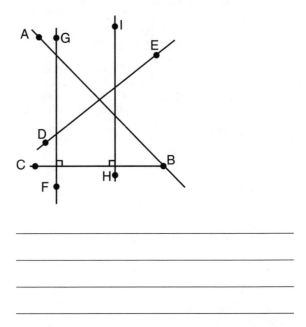

_____

_____

_____

_____

GO ON➡

36 What is the area of triangle DFG?
(Use $A = \frac{1}{2} bh$.)

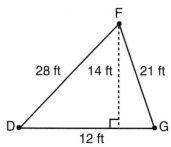

F 168 sq ft

G 84 sq ft

H 61 sq ft

J 49 sq ft

37 Larry wanted to bake granola bars for the club bake sale. Each batch took 1.5 cups of sugar. How many batches of granola bars could he make with a 3-quart container of sugar?

A 12

B 8

C 6

D 2

38 Which of the following metric units of measurement is best to use to measure the length of a room?

F meters

G liters

H centimeters

J kilograms

39 The picture shows that Toni is 10 yards from the tree. How many feet is that?

A 3 feet

B 30 feet

C 300 feet

D 3000 feet

40 For a history project, Jamie is making a scale drawing of the Washington Monument on a piece of posterboard that is $8\frac{1}{2}$ inches by 11 inches. If the monument is actually 555 feet high, what is a reasonable scale for her drawing?

F 1 in. represents 100 ft.

G 1 in. represents 10 ft.

H $\frac{1}{2}$ in. represents 1 ft.

J $\frac{1}{2}$ in. represents 10 ft.

41 The bus left the Dry Gulch Canyon bus station at 4:35 P.M. for a trip to Cherokee Flats that will take 2 hours and 50 minutes. At what time should the bus arrive at its destination?

_____

_____

_____

_____

_____

_____

_____

GO ON→

42 The sum of the first two numerals in Max's apartment number is twice the sum of the last two numerals. Which of these could be Max's apartment number?

A 842

B 824

C 428

D 248

43 According to this table, about how much taller is the Sears Tower than the Empire State Building?

World's Tallest Skyscrapers	
Building	Height
Amoco	1,136 feet
Empire State Building	1,250 feet
John Hancock Center	1,127 feet
Sears Tower	1,454 feet
World Trade Center	1,350 feet

F 100 feet

G 150 feet

H 200 feet

J 300 feet

44 Which of the following units of measurement is best to use to describe the weight of a box of breakfast cereal?

A feet

B ounces

C liters

D inches

45 Marco took a box of popsicles to the park. He ate one and gave one to each of 5 friends. What do you need to know to find out how many popsicles Marco has left?

F how many friends chose grape popsicles

G how many popsicles altogether were in the box

H how many boxes of popsicles Marco ate at home

J how many orange popsicles were in the box

46 The cost of a pound of coffee is $3.69. The Martinez family buys 1.5 pounds of coffee each week. The Goldsmith family buys 2.5 pounds of coffee each week. Which question below cannot be answered using the data given above?

A What is the total weight of the coffee bought by the two families?

B What is the difference between the amount of coffee bought by the Martinez and Goldsmith families?

C How much coffee remains unused by each family at the end of the week?

D What would be the total cost of coffee bought by both families in one week?

47 Nora took swimming lessons before beginning piano lessons. She joined gymnastics class after beginning piano lessons. She began dance class before beginning swimming lessons. Which lessons did she begin first?

_____

_____

_____

_____

_____

STOP

Sample A

Mr. Rafael uses his own truck at work. If he drove 128 miles last week, and 62 of those miles were for his personal use, how many miles did he drive on the job?

A 55 miles

B 58 miles

C 66 miles

D 190 miles

E NH

STOP

Sample B

196
× 9

F 954

G 1,764

H 1,954

J 9,764

K NH

STOP

For questions 1–14, darken the circle for the correct answer. If the correct answer is not given, darken the circle for NH (Not Here). If no choices are given, write in the answer.

1

208
× 14

A 2,812

B 2,912

C 2,922

D 3,912

E NH

2

$33\overline{)1746}$

F $22\frac{3}{11}$

G 52

H $52\frac{2}{11}$

J $52\frac{10}{11}$

K NH

3

706
× 80

A 56,480

B 56,408

C 56,068

D 5,648

E NH

4

$12\frac{1}{8}$
$+ 4\frac{1}{4}$

F $8\frac{1}{8}$

G $16\frac{1}{6}$

H $16\frac{3}{8}$

J $16\frac{3}{16}$

K NH

5

$1.758 \times 3.6 =$

A 0.63288

B 6.3288

C 63.288

D 632.88

E NH

6

$\frac{5}{6} \div \frac{2}{9} =$

F $3\frac{3}{4}$

G $4\frac{3}{4}$

H $\frac{5}{27}$

J $5\frac{2}{7}$

K NH

7

$8\frac{7}{8} - 3\frac{5}{6} =$

A $5\frac{1}{24}$

B $5\frac{1}{8}$

C $5\frac{3}{54}$

D $5\frac{3}{16}$

E NH

8

$0.9\overline{)0.72}$

F 8

G 0.8

H 0.08

J 0.008

K NH

GO ON

9 Tony brought a 132-ounce jug of a sports drink to football practice. If he wanted to share it equally with his 11 friends, how much would each person receive?

A 11 ounces

B 10 ounces

C 8 ounces

D 7 ounces

E NH

10 A paper company has two factories that produce cardboard boxes. Factory A produces $2\frac{3}{4}$ million boxes a year and Factory B produces $4\frac{2}{3}$ million boxes a year. What is the total cardboard box production for the company in one year?

F $7\frac{5}{12}$ million

G $7\frac{7}{12}$ million

H 8 million

J $8\frac{2}{3}$ million

K NH

11 Dominic bought 2 soccer balls for $39.45 each and a pair of soccer cleats for $44.99. Without including tax, how much did he spend altogether?

_____

_____

_____

_____

_____

12 Danielle and 5 of her friends won 108 six-packs of juice drinks in a radio promotional contest. How many six-packs of drinks should Danielle receive as her $\frac{1}{6}$ share?

A 11

B 12

C 16

D 18

E NH

13 Marty tests water samples for the state park department. This morning he is preparing to test water from Lost Hollow Stream. How many $2\frac{1}{2}$-liter beakers can Marty fill with the 15 liters of water he has collected from the stream?

F 12

G 8

H 6

J 37.5

K NH

14 Diane's craft club raised money by raffling a quilt the members had made. They raised $986 by selling tickets. The quilt cost $135 to make. How much profit did the club make?

_____

_____

_____

_____

STOP

LANGUAGE

Sample A

Shari is planning to write a letter to her community library to request that the library purchase books about hot-air balloons. Before she writes the letter, she wants to find the titles of some books on the subject. She is currently reading the book *Ballooning*. To help her find the titles of other books on ballooning, she should look in this book's—

A title page.

B bibliography.

C index.

D dictionary.

STOP

For questions 1–4, darken the circle for the correct answer, or write in the answer.

In social studies class, Paul was assigned to write a report on some aspect of the history of transportation. He decided to research sailing ships and use this as the subject of his report.

1 **What should Paul do before he writes his report?**

A think of some famous sailing ships to include in his report

B reread his report for errors in sentence structure

C make a list of topics to include in his report

D check a dictionary for spellings of words to include in his report

2 **What would Paul *not* want to include in his report?**

F a chapter on ancient sailboats

G the development of steamships

H a discussion of the importance of the change from square to triangular sails

J a chapter on famous sailing ships

3 **Where is the best place for Paul to find the most recent information about the design of modern sailing ships?**

A a newspaper

B the *Readers' Guide to Periodical Literature*

C a telephone directory

D an encyclopedia

4 **What method could Paul use to organize his thoughts before he writes his report?**

_____

_____

_____

_____

_____

GO ON

Here are the Table of Contents and the Index from a book Paul found on the history of sailing ships. Read them carefully. Then answer questions 5–9.

Table of Contents

Index

5 Which pages would have information on the voyages of the Golden Hind?

_____

_____

_____

6 Paul wanted to find information about explorers and the ships they used. All of these pages would be useful *except*—

F 40

G 42–45

H 55

J 28–30

7 Which chapter should Paul read to find the most information about the earliest kinds of sailing ships?

A Chapter 1

B Chapter 2

C Chapter 3

D Chapter 4

8 Which chapter should Paul read to find the most information about the ships used by Christopher Columbus when he landed in America?

F Chapter 3

G Chapter 4

H Chapter 5

J Chapter 6

9 Paul wanted to write a paragraph about a galleon used for fighting. On which pages could he probably find the most useful information on this topic?

_____

_____

_____

_____

_____

_____

_____

_____

GO ON ➡

Here is a rough draft of the first part of Paul's report. Read the rough draft carefully. Then answer questions 10–16.

The History of Sailing Ships

The origin thousands of years ago, sailing ships date back to. Historians believe
(1)   **(2)**

that the earliest civilization to use sailing ships was that of the ancient Egyptians.

The shape of the sail on the earliest sailing ships was square. A square-shaped
(3)   **(4)**

sail moved the earliest sailing ships. The mast, designed like a flagpole, held up
(5)

the sail. Papyrus, a fibrous reedlike plant, grows plentifully along the Nile
(6)

River. Besides being used to make a writing material, mats, and sandals,
(7)

papyrus was used to make the earliest sails. Surprisingly, this early type of
(8)

sailing ship is still used along the Nile in Egypt today. In the 1700s, most navies
(9)

in the world were known as fleets.

As time passed, the Egyptians change in their sailing ships. They reworked
(10)   **(11)**

the mast so it was shaped like a long narrow A. The mast was secured to the
(12)

ship with ropes. The boats by the crewmen who paddled them.
(13)

GO ON➡

10 Correctly rewrite sentence 1.

_____

_____

_____

_____

_____

_____

11 Which sentence needlessly repeats an idea?

A 2

B 3

C 4

D 5

12 Which of these sentences could be added after sentence 2?

F The Egyptians used these ships to sail the Nile River.

G The largest fighting ships, at this time, were made of iron.

H By 1900 sailing ships were mostly used for pleasure or sport.

J Why did people use sailing ships instead of steamboats?

13 Which sentence does _not_ belong in paragraph 2? Write the number.

_____

_____

_____

_____

14 What is the best way to write sentence 10?

A The Egyptians changed their sailing ships as time passed.

B As time passed, the Egyptians changes in their sailing ships made.

C As time passed, change in their sailing ships the Egyptians made.

D As it is written.

15 Which of these sentences could be added after sentence 12?

F Drawings of boats with sails have been found on early Egyptian pottery and on the walls of tombs.

G Greek ships sailed everywhere in the Mediterranean world, from the Black Sea in the east to Spain in the west.

H The ropes were lashed to the bow and to the stern of the ships.

J The Egyptian ships were used to transport papyrus to the interior of Africa for trade.

16 Which group of words is _not_ a complete sentence?

A 9

B 11

C 12

D 13

GO ON➡

Here is the next part of the rough draft of Paul's report. This part has certain words and phrases underlined. Read the draft carefully. Then answer questions 17–24.

The phoenician civilization was also known for its sailing ships. The powerful
(14)   (15)

Phoenicians were great sailors, traders navigators, and colonizers. They
                                        (16)

controlled the trade on the Mediterranean Sea. They also had a large fleet of
                                                                      (17)

sailing ships that were sturdy enough for the open seas of the Atlantic Ocean.

Phoenician ships had masts made from the timber of cedar trees and had
(18)

oars made of oak. In addition the boards for the hull were made from the timber
                              (19)

of fir trees. The hulls or frames of the sailing ships, were solidly built with ribs
              (20)

for extra support. The front and back of the hull was sharp curved upward for
                                                          (21)

faster, smoother sailing. Linen cloth from Egypt was used for the sails.
                                        (22)

Studying the construction of the earliest sailing ships makes people today
(23)

appreciate the skills of these early sailors. Anyone researching the history of
                                                          (24)

sailing ships were surprised at the seaworthiness of these early ships.

GO ON ➡

17 In sentence 14, <u>The phoenician civilization</u> is best written—

    F The Phoenician Civilization

    G The Phoenician civilization

    H the Phoenician civilization

    J As it is written.

18 In sentence 15, <u>sailors, traders navigators, and colonizers</u> is best written—

    A sailors, traders, navigators, and colonizers

    B sailors and traders, navigators, and colonizers

    C sailors and traders, and navigators and colonizers

    D As it is written.

19 In sentence 17, <u>They also had</u> is best written—

    F They also have

    G We also had

    H He and she also had

    J As it is written.

20 In sentence 19, <u>In addition the boards</u> is best written—

    A In addition the boards,

    B In addition, the boards,

    C In addition, the boards

    D As it is written.

21 In sentence 20, <u>hulls or frames of the sailing ships,</u> is best written—

    F hulls or frames of the sailing ships

    G hulls, or frames of the sailing ships,

    H hulls or frames, of the sailing ships

    J As it is written.

22 In sentence 21, <u>was sharp curved upward</u> is best written—

    A was sharp curve upward

    B was sharpest curve upward

    C were curved sharply upward

    D As it is written.

23 In sentence 23, <u>makes people today</u> is best written—

    F made people today

    G gives people today

    H has given people today

    J As it is written.

24 In sentence 24, <u>were surprised</u> is best written—

    A am surprised

    B will be surprised

    C will have been surprised

    D As it is written.

GO ON➡

For questions 25–36, read each sentence carefully. If one of the words is misspelled, darken the circle for that word. If all the words are spelled correctly, then darken the circle for *No mistake*.

25   She was <u>horse</u> from <u>cheering</u> after the team's big <u>victory</u>. <u>No mistake</u>
            F   G   H   J

26   I <u>dout</u> that the <u>package</u> will <u>arrive</u> today. <u>No mistake</u>
   A   B   C   D

27   Bill has <u>surffed</u> every <u>beach</u> on the northern <u>coast</u> of Hawaii. <u>No mistake</u>
           F   G   H   J

28   The actor's voice was <u>amplifyed</u> so he could be heard <u>throughout</u> the <u>theater</u>. <u>No mistake</u>
                     A   B   C   D

29   The Department of <u>Commerce</u> <u>imposed</u> a new <u>tariff</u> on certain foreign imports. <u>No mistake</u>
                    F   G   H   J

30   Her <u>house</u> is near the <u>intrasection</u> of Main Street and Willow <u>Avenue</u>. <u>No mistake</u>
   A   B   C   D

31   We have had very <u>unpleasant</u> <u>whether</u> <u>lately</u>. <u>No mistake</u>
                F   G   H   J

32   Muriel <u>wisked</u> the eggs well to make a <u>fluffy</u> <u>omelet</u>. <u>No mistake</u>
        A   B   C   D

33   Most <u>historians</u> consider Athens the <u>birthplace</u> of <u>democratcy</u>. <u>No mistake</u>
       F   G   H   J

34   The new budget <u>includes</u> a one-percent <u>increase</u> in sales <u>tacks</u>. <u>No mistake</u>
                A   B   C   D

35   My <u>physics</u> teacher <u>illustrated</u> her point by using a <u>transparentcy</u>. <u>No mistake</u>
       F   G   H   J

36   Juanita <u>practices</u> the <u>piano</u> for two hours every <u>afternoon</u>. <u>No mistake</u>
          A   B   C   D

STOP

ANSWER KEY

UNIT 2:
SIX READING SKILLS
p. 12 1. C 2. F 3. looking back
p. 13 1. A 2. J 3. burns
p. 14 1. C 2. G 3. prizes or loot
p. 15 1. D 2. G 3. B 4. F
p. 16 1. A 2. J 3. The Chinese kung fu experts turned back the Japanese with their bare hands.
p. 17 1. A 2. H 3. The younger son left home after his father and brother disappeared.
p. 18 1. A 2. J 3. He went back to the post office.
p. 19 1. C 2. H 3. The volcano erupted during the fall.
p. 20 1. C 2. H 3. how trees can be protected from deer
p. 21 1. A 2. F 3. Viruses have the power to kill despite their size.
pp. 22–23 1. B 2. G 3. B 4. H
p. 24 1. C 2. H 3. B 4. He had too much confidence.
p. 25 1. B 2. F 3. C 4. Sheila will probably go running.
pp. 26–27 1. A 2. May 13 would be the worst beach day because the temperature is low and the humidity is high. 3. F 4. The team's performance got worse for the 100m race.
p. 28 1. C 2. F 3. A 4. A nightmare awakened Charlene.
p. 29 1. A 2. H 3. D 4. Their problem got worse when they imported mongooses.
p. 30 1. C 2. J 3. A 4. Men and women have different habits.
p. 31 1. B 2. H 3. Bing's photos were mostly of people; Gilpin's photos were of scenery. 4. B 5. The women were tense and anxious.
pp. 32–33 1. C 2. H 3. Answers will vary. 4. D 5. J 6. reducing toxins, decontaminating food, longer shelf-life
p. 34 1. B 2. J 3. D 4. F
pp. 35–36 1. B 2. J 3. D 4. G 5. D 6. Spend more money to research edible plants.

UNIT 3:
READING COMPREHENSION
pp. 37–44 SA. C 1. B 2. The school wants students to sort and pack items and label boxes. 3. J 4. C 5. F 6. It stopped rattling its tail. 7. D 8. G 9. C 10. Emily learned to zip her tent at night. 11. H 12. D 13. F 14. This notice would most likely be found in a school newsletter. 15. D 16. J 17. C 18. The author's purpose is to give information about an outdoor education program. 19. G 20. C 21.
F 22. B 23. H 24. tennis court, wrist guard 25. Answers will vary. 26. C 27. H 28. by 1:00 on Sunday 29. C 30. J 31. You would most likely find this schedule in a local newspaper.
pp. 45–53 SA. C 1. D 2. F 3. The water is used to refill the car radiators when they boil over. 4. A 5. H 6. C 7. Answers will vary. 8. G 9. A 10. G 11. Answers will vary. 12. D 13. G 14. C 15. She became one of the 208 astronaut finalists. 16. H 17. B 18. G 19. Answers will vary. 20. C 21. J 22. C 23. H 24. The paintings on the wall in an Egyptian ruler's tomb show that he died from a bee sting. 25. B 26. F 27. B 28. The author wanted to inform readers about allergies. 29. G 30. A 31. G 32. C 33. F 34. She admires them for the way they treat their environment. 35. Jess decides to design a reusable bag for grocery stores.

UNIT 4:
READING VOCABULARY
p. 54 SA. B 1. C 2. G 3. A 4. J 5. D 6. F 7. C 8. H 9. D 10. F
p. 55 SA. A 1. D 2. H 3. B 4. H
p. 56 SA. B 1. C 2. G 3. A 4. loud or noisy 5. G 6. C 7. H 8. produce
pp. 57–59 SA. D 1. C 2. F 3. D 4. G 5. B 6. F 7. A 8. G 9. A SB. D 10. G 11. C 12. G 13. A 14. Answers will vary. SC. B 15. A 16. G 17. C 18. J 19. C 20. F 21. competent or efficient 22. noise

UNIT 5:
MATH PROBLEM-SOLVING PLAN
p. 61 **Step 1.** to determine the number of miles Justine drives to work in three weeks **Step 2.** She drives 20 miles one way Monday through Thursday and 50 miles one way on Friday. **Step 3.** Compute her driving distances. **Step 4.** 20 miles x 2 (for round-trip) x 4 = 160; 50 miles x 2 = 100; 160 + 100 = 260; 260 x 3 = 780 miles **Step 5.** Yes, because if the computations are correct, 780 miles is the number of miles she drove.
p. 62 **Step 1.** to determine on which day he spent the most money **Step 2.** On Monday he spent 1/2 of $48; on Tuesday he spent 1/3 of the remainder; on Wednesday he spent 1/4 of the remainder; on Thursday he spent 1/6 of the remainder.
Step 3. Compare numbers.
Step 4. On Monday, Ian spent the largest fraction of the largest amount. Therefore, it must be on Monday that he spent the greatest amount of money. **Step 5.** Yes, because the reasoning is sound.

UNIT 6:
MATH PROBLEM SOLVING
p. 63 SA. A 1. C 2. F 3. A 4. 5°
p. 64 SA. C 1. B 2. H 3. C 4. 2
p. 65 SA. B 1. C 2. J 3. A 4. J 5. $46.50
p. 66 SA. A 1. D 2. 20 3. H 4. B
pp. 67–68 SA. B 1. C 2. 188 3. J 4. C 5. F 6. B 7. F 8. B 9. $780
pp. 69–70 SA. D 1. A 2. 600 sq. ft. 3. H 4. B 5. F 6. C 7. J 8. D 9. radius
pp. 71–72 SA. C 1. D 2. H 3. 4 inches 4. D 5. H 6. B 7. F 8. D 9. 18 feet 10. 45 minutes
p. 73 SA. C 1. D 2. 30 3. G 4. 42, 44, 46, 48, 50, 52
p. 74 SA. B 1. D 2. H 3. C 4. G 5. 3,000 miles
pp. 75–80 SA. C 1. B 2. G 3. A 4. H 5. C 6. G 7. All are multiples of 3. 8. C 9. J 10. 40 11. B 12. J 13. D 14. F 15. C 16. F 17. narrow tip 18. B 19. J 20. C 21. H 22. A 23. H 24. line segment AC 25. D 26. G 27. D 28. H 29. 8:09 30. C 31. J 32. 12 33. B 34. 35 miles 35. H 36. C 37. G 38. A
p. 81 SA. C 1. E 2. G 3. A 4. F 5. B 6. J
p. 82 SA. C 1. A 2. H 3. C 4. H
pp. 83–84 SA. E SB. H 1. B 2. F 3. A 4. H 5. A 6. H 7. C 8. 201,210 9. H 10. C 11. F 12. D 13. H 14. $2.34

UNIT 7:
LANGUAGE
pp. 85–90 SA. B 1. C 2. G 3. D 4. F 5. A 6. Chapter 6 7. H 8. A 9. G 10. D 11. J 12. The coral remains in this home for life. 13. D 14. G 15. A 16. Lagoons, shallow ponds with no place to hide, are dangerous places for colorful fish. 17. G 18. C 19. H 20. It protects itself from predators by using poison.
p. 91 SA. D 1. D 2. G 3. A 4. G 5. A 6. G 7. A 8. F
pp. 92–96 SA. C 1. D 2. He wants to learn more about the Olympic Games. 3. G 4. A 5. H 6. 10 7. A 8. G 9. their 10. A 11. J 12. C 13. C 14. B 15. H 16. B 17. H 18. D 19. F 20. B

21. F 22. A 23. J 24. C

UNIT 8:
PRACTICE TEST 1:
READING COMPREHENSION
pp. 97–105 SA. D 1. B 2. F 3. B 4. G 5. C 6. F 7. D 8. Answers will vary. 9. F 10. B 11. Pete 12. G 13. C 14. J 15. C 16. It was a picture of everything she dreamed of and cherished. 17. J 18. C 19. F 20. Devotion and kindness are rewarded; selfishness and greed are punished. 21. C 22. G 23. D 24. J 25. A 26. F 27. army service 28. A 29. G 30. B 31. H 32. A 33. Sample answer: to show that the company really believes in its bicycle.

UNIT 9:
PRACTICE TEST 2:
READING VOCABULARY
pp. 106–108 SA. C 1. C 2. H 3. D 4. G 5. B 6. J 7. A 8. G SB. C 9. C 10. H 11. C 12. J 13. B SC. A 14. H 15. B 16. H 17. defect 18. D 19. G 20. A 21. astonished

UNIT 10:
PRACTICE TEST 3
PART 1:
MATH PROBLEM SOLVING
pp. 109–116 SA. C 1. A 2. J 3. 5° 4. A 5. F 6. B 7. F 8. B 9. 8 10. H 11. C 12. H 13. C 14. J 15. D 16. 4 x 10 17. G 18. A 19. 24 20. F 21. D 22. Sales dropped slightly, then rose sharply. 23. H 24. $100 25. B 26. G 27. A 28. $117 29. J 30. D 31. G 32. D 33. G 34. A 35. line segments GF and IH 36. G 37. B 38. F 39. B 40. F 41. 7:25 PM 42. A 43. H 44. B 45. G 46. C 47. dance lessons

PART 2:
MATH PROCEDURES
pp. 117–118 SA. C SB. G 1. B 2. J 3. A 4. H 5. B 6. F 7. A 8. G 9. E 10. F 11. $123.89 12. D 13. H 14. $851

UNIT 11:
PRACTICE TEST 4:
LANGUAGE
pp. 119–124 SA. B 1. C 2. G 3. B 4. Make a concept web showing the history of sailing ships. 5. 70 and 72 6. J 7. A 8. G 9. 61–64, 67 10. The origin of sailing dates back thousands of years. 11. C 12. F 13. 9 14. A 15. H 16. D 17. G 18. A 19. J 20. C 21. G 22. C 23. J 24. B 25. F 26. A 27. F 28. A 29. J 30. B 31. G 32. A 33. H 34. C 35. H 36. D

Answer Sheet

STUDENT'S NAME			SCHOOL:

LAST — **FIRST** — **MI**

TEACHER:

FEMALE ○   MALE ○

Name grid columns (each column has: ○ A B C D E F G H I J K L M N O P Q R S T U V W X Y Z)

BIRTH DATE

MONTH		DAY		YEAR	
Jan ○		⓪	⓪	⓪	⓪
Feb ○		①	①	①	①
Mar ○		②	②	②	②
Apr ○		③	③	③	③
May ○			④	④	④
Jun ○			⑤	⑤	⑤
Jul ○			⑥	⑥	⑥
Aug ○			⑦	⑦	⑦
Sep ○			⑧	⑧	⑧
Oct ○			⑨	⑨	⑨
Nov ○					
Dec ○					

GRADE ④ ⑤ ⑥ ⑦ ⑧

Fill in the circle for each multiple-choice answer. Write the answers to the open-ended questions on a separate sheet of paper.

TEST 1   Reading Comprehension

SA Ⓐ Ⓑ Ⓒ Ⓓ   6 Ⓕ Ⓖ Ⓗ Ⓙ   12 Ⓕ Ⓖ Ⓗ Ⓙ   18 Ⓐ Ⓑ Ⓒ Ⓓ   24 Ⓕ Ⓖ Ⓗ Ⓙ   30 Ⓐ Ⓑ Ⓒ Ⓓ
1 Ⓐ Ⓑ Ⓒ Ⓓ   7 Ⓐ Ⓑ Ⓒ Ⓓ   13 Ⓐ Ⓑ Ⓒ Ⓓ   19 Ⓕ Ⓖ Ⓗ Ⓙ   25 Ⓐ Ⓑ Ⓒ Ⓓ   31 Ⓕ Ⓖ Ⓗ Ⓙ
2 Ⓕ Ⓖ Ⓗ Ⓙ   8 OPEN ENDED   14 Ⓕ Ⓖ Ⓗ Ⓙ   20 OPEN ENDED   26 Ⓕ Ⓖ Ⓗ Ⓙ   32 Ⓐ Ⓑ Ⓒ Ⓓ
3 Ⓐ Ⓑ Ⓒ Ⓓ   9 Ⓕ Ⓖ Ⓗ Ⓙ   15 Ⓐ Ⓑ Ⓒ Ⓓ   21 Ⓐ Ⓑ Ⓒ Ⓓ   27 OPEN ENDED   33 OPEN ENDED
4 Ⓕ Ⓖ Ⓗ Ⓙ   10 Ⓐ Ⓑ Ⓒ Ⓓ   16 OPEN ENDED   22 Ⓕ Ⓖ Ⓗ Ⓙ   28 Ⓐ Ⓑ Ⓒ Ⓓ
5 Ⓐ Ⓑ Ⓒ Ⓓ   11 OPEN ENDED   17 Ⓕ Ⓖ Ⓗ Ⓙ   23 Ⓐ Ⓑ Ⓒ Ⓓ   29 Ⓕ Ⓖ Ⓗ Ⓙ

TEST 2   Reading Vocabulary

SA Ⓐ Ⓑ Ⓒ Ⓓ   4 Ⓕ Ⓖ Ⓗ Ⓙ   8 Ⓕ Ⓖ Ⓗ Ⓙ   11 Ⓐ Ⓑ Ⓒ Ⓓ   14 Ⓕ Ⓖ Ⓗ Ⓙ   18 Ⓐ Ⓑ Ⓒ Ⓓ
1 Ⓐ Ⓑ Ⓒ Ⓓ   5 Ⓐ Ⓑ Ⓒ Ⓓ   SB Ⓐ Ⓑ Ⓒ Ⓓ   12 Ⓕ Ⓖ Ⓗ Ⓙ   15 Ⓐ Ⓑ Ⓒ Ⓓ   19 Ⓕ Ⓖ Ⓗ Ⓙ
2 Ⓕ Ⓖ Ⓗ Ⓙ   6 Ⓕ Ⓖ Ⓗ Ⓙ   9 Ⓐ Ⓑ Ⓒ Ⓓ   13 Ⓐ Ⓑ Ⓒ Ⓓ   16 Ⓕ Ⓖ Ⓗ Ⓙ   20 Ⓐ Ⓑ Ⓒ Ⓓ
3 Ⓐ Ⓑ Ⓒ Ⓓ   7 Ⓐ Ⓑ Ⓒ Ⓓ   10 Ⓕ Ⓖ Ⓗ Ⓙ   SC Ⓐ Ⓑ Ⓒ Ⓓ   17 OPEN ENDED   21 OPEN ENDED

TEST 3   **Part 1: Math Problem Solving**

SA (A) (B) (C) (D)	8 (A) (B) (C) (D)	16 OPEN ENDED	24 OPEN ENDED	32 (A) (B) (C) (D)	40 (F) (G) (H) (J)
1 (A) (B) (C) (D)	9 OPEN ENDED	17 (F) (G) (H) (J)	25 (A) (B) (C) (D)	33 (F) (G) (H) (J)	41 OPEN ENDED
2 (F) (G) (H) (J)	10 (F) (G) (H) (J)	18 (A) (B) (C) (D)	26 (F) (G) (H) (J)	34 (A) (B) (C) (D)	42 (A) (B) (C) (D)
3 OPEN ENDED	11 (A) (B) (C) (D)	19 OPEN ENDED	27 (A) (B) (C) (D)	35 OPEN ENDED	43 (F) (G) (H) (J)
4 (A) (B) (C) (D)	12 (F) (G) (H) (J)	20 (F) (G) (H) (J)	28 OPEN ENDED	36 (F) (G) (H) (J)	44 (A) (B) (C) (D)
5 (F) (G) (H) (J)	13 (A) (B) (C) (D)	21 (A) (B) (C) (D)	29 (F) (G) (H) (J)	37 (A) (B) (C) (D)	45 (F) (G) (H) (J)
6 (A) (B) (C) (D)	14 (F) (G) (H) (J)	22 OPEN ENDED	30 (A) (B) (C) (D)	38 (F) (G) (H) (J)	46 (A) (B) (C) (D)
7 (F) (G) (H) (J)	15 (A) (B) (C) (D)	23 (F) (G) (H) (J)	31 (F) (G) (H) (J)	39 (A) (B) (C) (D)	47 OPEN ENDED

Part 2: Math Procedures

SA (A) (B) (C) (D) (E)	2 (F) (G) (H) (J) (K)	5 (A) (B) (C) (D) (E)	8 (F) (G) (H) (J) (K)	11 OPEN ENDED	14 OPEN ENDED
SB (F) (G) (H) (J) (K)	3 (A) (B) (C) (D) (E)	6 (F) (G) (H) (J) (K)	9 (A) (B) (C) (D) (E)	12 (A) (B) (C) (D) (E)	
1 (A) (B) (C) (D) (E)	4 (F) (G) (H) (J) (K)	7 (A) (B) (C) (D) (E)	10 (F) (G) (H) (J) (K)	13 (F) (G) (H) (J) (K)	

TEST 4   Language

SA (A) (B) (C) (D)	8 (F) (G) (H) (J)	16 (A) (B) (C) (D)	24 (A) (B) (C) (D)	32 (A) (B) (C) (D)
1 (A) (B) (C) (D)	9 OPEN ENDED	17 (F) (G) (H) (J)	25 (F) (G) (H) (J)	33 (F) (G) (H) (J)
2 (F) (G) (H) (J)	10 OPEN ENDED	18 (A) (B) (C) (D)	26 (A) (B) (C) (D)	34 (A) (B) (C) (D)
3 (A) (B) (C) (D)	11 (A) (B) (C) (D)	19 (F) (G) (H) (J)	27 (F) (G) (H) (J)	35 (F) (G) (H) (J)
4 (F) (G) (H) (J)	12 (F) (G) (H) (J)	20 (A) (B) (C) (D)	28 (A) (B) (C) (D)	36 (A) (B) (C) (D)
5 (A) (B) (C) (D)	13 OPEN ENDED	21 (F) (G) (H) (J)	29 (F) (G) (H) (J)	
	14 (A) (B) (C) (D)	22 (A) (B) (C) (D)	30 (A) (B) (C) (D)	
	15 (F) (G) (H) (J)	23 (F) (G) (H) (J)	31 (F) (G) (H) (J)	